A Student's Guide to

ERNEST
HEMINGWAY

UNDERSTANDING LITERATURE

A Student's Guide to

ERNEST HEMINGWAY

Timothy J. Pingelton

Enslow Publishers, Inc.

40 Industrial Road	PO Box 38
Box 398	Aldershot
Berkeley Heights, NJ 07922	Hants GU12 6BP
USA	UK

http://www.enslow.com

Library of Congress Cataloging-in-Publication Data

Pingelton, Timothy J.
    A student's guide to Ernest Hemingway / Timothy J. Pingelton.
        p. cm. — (Understanding literature)
        Includes bibliographical references and index.
        ISBN 0-7660-2431-8
        1. Hemingway, Ernest, 1899–1961—Examinations—Study guides—
Juvenile literature. 2. Authors, American—20th century—Biography—
Examinations—Study guides—Juvenile literature. 3. Journalists—United
States—Biography—Examinations—Study guides—Juvenile literature. I. Title.
II. Series.
    PS3515.E37Z75415 2005
    813'.52—dc22
                              2004026102

Printed in the United States of America

10 9 8 7 6 5 4 3 2 1

To Our Readers:
We have done our best to make sure all Internet addresses in this book were active
and appropriate when we went to press. However, the author and the publisher
have no control over and assume no liability for the material available on those
Internet sites or on other Web sites they may link to. Any comments or suggestions
can be sent by e-mail to comments@enslow.com or to the address on the back
cover.

Illustration Credits: Enslow Publishers, Inc., p. 38; Library of Congress,
p. 99; all other images courtesy of the Ernest Hemingway Collection, John
Fitzgerald Kennedy Library.

Cover Illustration: Courtesy of the Ernest Hemingway Collection,
John Fitzgerald Kennedy Library (inset); Corel Corporation/Hemera
Technologies, Inc. (background objects).

Dedication

To Sophie—one heck of a gal.

CONTENTS

CHAPTER 1

THE LOST GENERATION

An Introduction to the Life and Works of Ernest Hemingway

In many ways, the writing and life of Ernest Hemingway could be seen as a bridge. This bridge connects such concepts as Old World and New World, Victorian and Modern, Romanticism and Realism, traditional and cutting-edge, peace and war, sacred and profane, country and city, life and death.

In one of his most famous short stories, "A Clean, Well-Lighted Place," an old waiter tries to explain to a young waiter how opposites like these can work together. The young waiter cannot understand these things because he has not lived long enough to understand. Their conversation takes place late at night, between night and day. It is very dark outside, but the café is full of light. The ideas of the old waiter and the young waiter, day and night, dark and light mix in this story, and the reader is left to think about how to interpret them. Much of Hemingway's writing carries this mix in it, forming a unique tone and texture.

THE VICTORIAN ERA

Ernest Hemingway was born in the Victorian era. The Victorian era ended in 1901, when Queen Victoria died. It was a time of great literature by Charles Dickens, Emily Brontë, and Lord Tennyson. Roughly speaking, these writers produced works about how the individual person acts in society, how old ideas can survive with new science, and the failure of traditional ways of looking at things.

Hemingway's writing carries much of the Victorian style, but his works bridge to modernism and beyond. Modernism broke from old ways of thinking and writing in order to explore new forms. Literature of this period strove to write about

VICTORIAN ERA— *Time spanning the reign of Queen Victoria (1837–1901), a long era of writing that saw works moving away from moral righteousness. The late part of this era saw literature that explored the struggle between the rich and the poor, religion and science.*

life as it really is, without the happy endings or unreal characters popular in earlier periods. This kind of writing shocked some people and appealed to others.

FORMS OF MODERNISM

MODERNISM— *In literature, an era when writers wanted to break from the style of the past to explore new ways of writing. The movement is a little different in Europe and America, but it could be said to span from 1900 to 1960.*

There are different types of modernism. In general modernism does not focus on leaders or famous people. It is about common people in common situations. These characters usually have some kind of flaw. They are usually from somewhere other than where they are in the book or story, and they are not sure what they can believe in. Things that once seemed certain to these characters are now uncertain.

In his writing, Ernest Hemingway uses ideas from the Bible, from Shakespeare, from low-life and high-life people he met, and from other writers and artists. He remembered people and events and used them later in his poetry, stories, and novels. Some things he wrote seem better than they were, and some things he wrote seem worse than they were.

ROMANCE TO REALISM

Hemingway bridged romanticism and realism. Romantic writers were inspired by medieval stories of brave knights (such as the stories of King Arthur) as well as newer stories in which the hero saves the damsel in distress. In short, romantic literature is fiction in which life is made to seem perfect and the ending is usually happy. Common life is not the focus of these stories. There will be a small problem, but the hero will solve the problem. The popularity of this kind of writing faded toward the end of the 1800s.

ROMANTIC LITERATURE— *Writing that emphasizes passion and imagination over realism.*

As more and more people in Europe and America moved to cities and worked in large factories toward the end of the nineteenth century, literature about mysterious perfect places became less popular. Realism became more interesting to readers. Realism is writing that observes without emotion or without making things perfect. A romantic writer might look at a tree and make it seem like that tree is the perfect tree. The realist writer would factually describe its size, color, and properties. The realist would describe the flaws as well as the beautiful parts. Most writing these days falls in the category of realism.

REALISM— *Writing that emphasizes people and situations that are more true to life.*

Here is an example of Hemingway's realism from the beginning of his story "In Another Country":

> It was cold in the fall in Milan and the dark came very early. Then the electric lights came on, and it was pleasant along the streets looking in the windows. There was much game hanging outside the shops, and the snow powdered in the fur of the foxes and the wind blew their tails. The deer hung stiff and heavy and empty, and small birds blew in the wind and the wind turned their feathers. It was a cold fall and the wind came down from the mountain.[1]

This description is very factual and direct. He describes the animals hanging outside the shops in Milan, Italy, without using very many (if any) adjectives.

The foxes tails are not described as bushy or soft. We know it is cold, but Hemingway does not use words like "freezing cold" or "bitterly cold" to describe the coldness. This realism and factual (or "objective") style is seen throughout nearly all of Hemingway's writing.

INFLUENCES ON HEMINGWAY

Hemingway was a big reader. It seems he was always reading a book when he had free time. When he was in high school, he tried to write in the style of Ring Lardner. Lardner wrote humorous short stories, many times about sports. The young Ernest Hemingway wrote for the school newspaper in high school. He also thought Joseph Conrad, author of the book *Heart of Darkness*, was a great writer. By reading so much, Hemingway learned the difference between good and bad writing. He also learned how to write without sounding fake.

Ernest Hemingway was also influenced by the visual arts. He liked the paintings of Joan Miró, Pablo Picasso, and Paul Cézanne. He thought these painters were better artists than artists who painted things just as they look. The painters he liked painted how things *feel*. They used color and light to show more than a person can see. They gave their subjects emotion. After he left home, Hemingway wrote his friend Gertrude Stein that he was trying to write like Cézanne painted.

"A LOST GENERATION"

In his novel *A Moveable Feast*, published three years after his death, Ernest Hemingway tells the story of how he and his peers acquired the name The Lost Generation. Hemingway often visited American writer Gertrude Stein in the early 1920s when they were living in separate parts of Paris. He went to Ms. Stein's apartment for writing advice and to talk about art. In her apartment, she had several original paintings by artists such as Cézanne. Once he accompanied Ms. Stein to get her car repaired. The mechanic was very slow in getting the Model A repaired, and his boss scolded him. Ms. Stein overheard the mechanic's boss and used what the boss said to describe Hemingway.

"That's what you are. That's what you all are," Miss Stein said. "All of you young people who served in the war. You are a lost generation."[2] Hemingway thought that was a very interesting thing to say, and he used this as the epigram to his novel *The Sun Also Rises*.

Although Ernest Hemingway did not eagerly embrace the

> **THE LOST GENERATION—** *A group of writers who gained fame between World War I and the 1930s. They wrote about the rootlessness, futility, and alienation they felt.*

term, the Lost Generation has come to signify a group of American writers whose writing career began in the decade or two following World War I. These writers (F. Scott Fitzgerald, e. e. cummings, John Dos Passos, Hart Crane, and others) found the world after the terrible war to be without justice or faith. The previous generation's values were lost in this new cold, unpredictable, and unfeeling world. Values inherited from their parents and grandparents remained, but the Lost Generation had to change the values to fit the new world. Advances in science, technology, warfare, and the development of a global rather than solely American outlook made the era between World War I and World War II a time of testing values and changing what did not seem to work.

For example, many in the Lost Generation believed that a person could be religious without always going to church. Hemingway's character Nick Adams uses the rituals of setting up camp and fishing on the river in the same way some people use the rituals of a church service. Also, many in the Lost Generation thought one person exploring his or her beliefs was more important than following the beliefs of a group.

For example, the large number of American

writers who fought in the Spanish Civil War (1936–1939) fought not for the needs of a country but because they personally wanted fascism to be stopped. Fascism is a political movement in which the

> **FASCISM**—*A type of government that encourages nationalism over individuality. A severe leader silences anyone who speaks against the government.*

nation is more important than individual people. Usually a fascist government has a powerful leader who forces people to do what he wants them to do rather than what is actually good for them. In fascism, people are not allowed to speak out against the government.

Many of these American writers left America and came to Europe (mainly Paris) to enjoy a society that, to them, seemed more worldly, cultured, and relaxed. Very few of these expatriates gave up U.S. citizenship, but they all felt a kind of betrayal by the country many of them had fought for in World War I. Also, it was easier for writers and other artists to live as artists in Paris because the exchange rate was very favorable to Americans. This lifestyle typically included lingering over long meals at sidewalk cafés, drinking alcohol, and traveling. In the 1920s and 1930s America was going through very bad economic times, and Paris was more easy-going. For Hemingway, this period in Paris inspired his work as a poet, short-story writer, and novelist.

WRITING WHAT CANNOT BE WRITTEN

Ernest Hemingway wrote about what he knew. He served (to some extent) in three major wars, and he wrote about war. He was married four times, and he wrote about love. He attended numerous bullfights, and he wrote about bull-fighting. He was an outdoorsman, and he wrote about the outdoors. Although Nick Adams, the character who appears in many of Hemingway's short stories, has many of the same experiences Hemingway had in real life, Hemingway tells you this indirectly. For example, rather than say that Nick Adams was in the war before coming to fish the Big, Two-Hearted River, Hemingway has him set up camp, prepare a meal, and think in such a way as to let the clever reader learn that he was in the war.

Hemingway believed that a good writer can express deep ideas without ruining the mood of a story by having the writer directly tell the

Ernest Hemingway is pictured here during his early years in Paris, circa 1923.

reader what to think. The clever writer can show the emotion of a situation by detailing what a character does or how he or she interacts with other characters.

Although much of Hemingway's writing is alive with action, some stories or sections of novels appear to be nothing more than description of a common event or action. In these sections, Hemingway is attempting to create, in as few words as possible, a certain emotion in the reader. After being involved in an interesting experience, his mentor Gertrude Stein advised him, "Find what gave you the emotion; what the action was that gave you the excitement. Then write it down making it clear so the reader will see it too and have the same feeling that you had."[3] Telling readers something specific is difficult, but making readers feel the emotion you want them to feel can only be accomplished by the very best writers.

IRONY AND PITY

In *The Sun Also Rises*, the novel that established Ernest Hemingway as a serious writer, two characters are joining around over breakfast. Bill starts singing a silly song:

> As I went down-stairs I heard Bill singing, "Irony and Pity. When you're feeling . . . Oh, Give then Irony and Give them Pity. [...]"
> "What's all this irony and pity?"
> "What? Don't you know about Irony and Pity?"
> "No. Who got it up?"
> "Everybody. They're mad about it in New York."[4]

IRONY—*(1) When a word or words are used to express an idea that is opposite that of the words' literal meaning. (2) When the expected outcome is different from what actually happens.*

Here, Hemingway is making fun of people who think any novel with irony and pity is a good novel. Irony is a very old writing device. When the speaker means the opposite of what he or she says, the speaker is being ironic. Also, when what actually happens is different from what is expected, that is ironic. Writers of the Lost Generation wrote about scenes with irony because they believed that what is expected may or may not happen. It cannot be controlled. These writers, however, did not treat irony as a joke, as Bill in *The Sun Also Rises* does.

Pity means feeling sadness or compassion for someone in trouble. Several writers of

Hemingway's generation felt pity for the Spanish people who were forced out of their homes by fascists. Once again, pity was a serious feeling; it was not something a writer could just add to a book to make it better. There may be much irony and pity in Hemingway's writing, but it is not used merely to sell more books. Irony and pity arise from Hemingway's writing because he felt he was trying to write about the truth. Hemingway was not satisfied to merely tell his readers about events; he wanted readers to visualize the events and feel the emotions of the characters.

WRITING WITHOUT WORDS

Another facet of the Lost Generation was their dislike for clichés and overblown, flowery language. They avoided any word that had lost its true meaning. For example, can a writer really define "love" for all readers? "Love" can mean many different things. Hemingway wrote, "Abstract words such as glory, honor, courage, or hallow were obscene beside the concrete names of villages, the numbers of roads, the names of rivers, the numbers of regiments and the dates."[5]

Rather than telling what "love" is in limited words, he showed what "love" is by showing one person sacrificing for another. Hemingway said he strove to create a true and artistic landscape using words in the way French painter Paul Cézanne used oil paint.

THE SHORT, DECLARATIVE SENTENCE

As a reporter for the Kansas City *Star*, Hemingway learned the newspaper's writing style. The editor urged journalists to writer clearly and simply, using as few words as possible. A good writer uses all five of his or her senses in writing—sight, hearing, smell, touch, and taste. The facts of an event are mixed with the writer's impressions or feelings about the event. This forces the writer to find the perfect word and not fill the page with unnecessary, distracting words. Journalism is at the root of Ernest Hemingway's writing, and the techniques he learned at the Kansas City *Star* and other publications were practiced throughout his life.

Hemingway's stories are full of simple sentences that carry much weight. The first sentence of "Big, Two-Hearted River" is this: "The train went on up the track out of sight, around one of the hills of burnt timber."[6] It appears to be a simple sentence describing a simple scene, but after carefully reading the whole story, that simple sentence reveals strong emotions.

Nick Adams, the character in the story, is left in the wild. The train is a symbol for the modern world. The wilderness is uncivilized, wild, and a memory from Nick's past. "He felt he had left everything behind, the need for thinking, the need to write, other needs. It was all back to him."[7] Even the town that used to be where Nick is has been burned to the ground. Nick knew the area when old buildings still stood along the one street of the small town. Things have changed, and now he is returning to nature. More than the little town has changed, however. The careful reader finds out that Nick has changed. It will be interesting how Nick handles things now that the train has pulled out of sight. The land is not the same, and he is not the same.

Life and emotions are complex. Ernest Hemingway writes about the complexities of life, but he writes about them in simple, straightforward language. Hemingway poured an incredible amount of effort into his writing, but he left much work for the reader. Although Hemingway uses simple words and sentences, the reader must constantly ask, "Why did that character do that?" or "Why is the timber burnt?" It may take some thought to find an answer, but that answer will prove to be much bigger than the little sentence it came from.

'FRAID A NOTHING!

The Roots and Development of Hemingway's Writing

Ernest Miller Hemingway was born on July 21, 1899, in Oak Park, Illinois. His mother, Grace, wanted to be an opera singer, but instead she managed the house and gave music lessons. His father, Clarence, was a medical doctor who enjoyed fishing and studying the outdoors. Ernest Hemingway's grandfathers Anson T. Hemingway and Ernest Hall were both Civil War veterans. Clarence and Grace were very religious and strict parents. His parents also taught Ernest and his older sister Marcelline how to have fun in nature.

When Ernest was only one year old, his parents took him to their vacation house in northern Michigan, on Walloon Lake. There, the young boy showed an interest in outdoor activities. He loved to ride in the family rowboat and eat fish caught by his father. He carried these interests throughout his life. Ernest and his family returned to northern Michigan for many summers.

GROWING UP

As a toddler, Hemingway showed no fear of exploring the lake property. There is a family story of Hemingway tripping while running with a stick in his mouth one summer. The stick poked the back of his throat, and his father had to act fast to take care of the serious wound. This was one of many serious injuries he would face in his lifetime. At age five, when Ernest was asked what he was afraid of, he answered, "'fraid a nothing!"[1]

Ernest Hemingway had three younger sisters—Ursula, Madelaine, and Carol—and a younger brother, Leicester. It seems he gave almost everyone in the Hemingway family a nickname. Ernest called himself Pawnee Bill or Nurnie, Ursula was called Mr. Gigs, Madelaine was called Sunny, Leicester was called The Pest, and his grandfather

A five-year-old Ernest Hemingway already demonstrates a passion for fishing.

Ernest was called Abba Bear. Years later, he gave his own children interesting nicknames.

Clarence Hemingway established the Oak Park, Illinois, Agassiz Club. This was an organization that taught boys about nature and Christianity. While the local boys were out on an expedition to study moss or mushrooms, Clarence Hemingway taught them that all things are created by God and that God is more powerful than any other force. These ideas can be found in Hemingway's writing.

A story he wrote titled "A Natural History of the Dead" contains the tale of Mungo Park. He was an adventurer who found himself wandering across an African desert, thirsty, naked, and about to die. Then Park saw a tiny flower growing in the sand. He thought that since God put that flower there and made sure it lived, then God would want him to live too. Park forced himself to keep on walking, and he at last came to a village and was saved.

Then, in the story, Hemingway compares the tale of Mungo Park to the tale of a person studying people killed in war. The tiny flower inspired Mungo Park to survive, but studying the dead leads the observer to think that war is unnatural

Grace Hemingway and her children, Ernest, Ursula, and Marcelline (left to right), admire a fish they caught during an outing on Walloon Lake in 1904.

and terrible. In the Agassiz "classes" Clarence Hemingway taught, the boys thought like Mungo Park. War is made by humans and not by nature. Nature is to be admired, and humans are to be feared. The idea that people are not perfect and are sometimes very bad appears in many of Hemingway's stories and books.

School Days

In school, Ernest Hemingway showed an early interest in reading and writing. He read everything from William Shakespeare, Jack London, and Mark Twain to articles in the newspaper. He also started writing short stories based on what his grandfather Anson told him and what he experienced in Michigan. Although Ernest had a hard time in his Latin and math classes, his English teachers praised his enthusiasm. He also wrote for his school newspaper.

Ernest Hemingway was also a good athlete. He joined the high school track, swimming, and football teams. On the weekends, he loved hunting, hiking, and working out with boxers. When he was a senior in high school, Ernest

The Hemingway children circa 1915 (from right to left): Marcelline, Ernest, Ursula, Madelaine, Carol, and Leicester.

Hemingway weighed 150 pounds and was nearly six feet tall.

After graduation from high school, Ernest's father wanted him to go to college, but Ernest was not sure. The year was 1917, and World War I (then called The Great War) was raging in Europe. By 1917 signs of the war had made it to Oak Park, Illinois. Ernest thought about fighting in Europe, and he thought about taking a job as a reporter for The Kansas City *Star*—at that time one of the largest newspapers in the country. Dr. Hemingway did not want his son to enter the war at such a young age (eighteen), and talked with Ernest's uncle Tyler, who lived in Kansas City, about arranging a job interview for Ernest.

WORLD WAR I

World War I began in June of 1914 when Archduke Francis Ferdinand of Austria was assassinated by a man with ties to a Serbian terrorist group. This led Austria to declare war on Serbia. Other European nations quickly chose sides and the conflict grew rapidly. The U.S. entered the war in 1917, after German subs began sinking unarmed American ships. While each side expected a quick victory, the war lasted more than four years and took the lives of nearly 10 million people.

STAR COPY STYLE

Ernest chose to move to Kansas City. He loved working as a reporter for a big-city newspaper.

The Hemingway family home in Oak Park, Illinois. Ernest Hemingway left home at age eighteen, shortly after graduating high school.

He worked long hours and wrote stories about criminals and celebrities. Much of what he saw as a reporter would be used in stories much later in his life. It was at the *Star* where Ernest Hemingway formed his writing style.

Working as a reporter for just over six months, Hemingway crafted the writing style that would make him famous. Each reporter was given a copy of "The *Star* Copy Style," which listed the rules for how to write for the newspaper. For example, here are the first four rules: "Use short sentences. Use short first paragraphs. Use vigorous English. Be positive, not negative."[2] There are dozens of other rules. Another rule is "Avoid using *that* too frequently, but govern use largely by euphony, and strive for smoothness." This means to write so it *sounds* smooth; euphony means what sounds good. While he did not follow all these rules in his stories, he did learn how to choose the best word and how to say a lot with only a few words.

Read the following paragraph. Think about what the scene would be like if you were there, right where the story takes place.

> At this time we were working in a shell-smashed house that overlooked the Casa del Campo in

Madrid. Below us a battle was being fought. You could see it spread out below you and over the hills, could smell it, could taste the dust of it, and the noise of it was one great slithering sheet of rifle and automatic rifle fire rising and dropping, and in it came the crack of the guns and the bubbly rumbling of the ongoing shells fired from the batteries behind us, the thud of their bursts, and then the rolling yellow clouds of dust."[3]

Hemingway writes "you," implying that you, the reader, could be included. This gets the reader involved with the story. He tells us what we can see, smell, taste, and hear.

Instead of writing that a terrible battle was going on, he puts us in the battle and shows us what it is like. Also, by writing "at this time," he lets us know that the storyteller has been in other situations like this.

Putting these things together, the reader can more easily imagine being in this story. Getting the reader into the story makes the reader care more about what happens.

Hemingway wants you to feel uncomfortable, because he wants you to realize that war is dirty, terrible, and scary. He learned this writing style by working as a newspaper reporter.

WINDS OF WAR

In the spring of 1918, after the U.S. had entered World War I, Ernest Hemingway got on a train headed for Chicago and then on to New York. Hemingway had enlisted in the Italian Red Cross to serve as an ambulance driver in Italy. Like the United States, Italy was fighting against Germany. His parents were worried about him, but they thought that he would be carrying out Christian duties, so they supported him.

Hemingway saw terrible sights in Italy as an ambulance driver. After about one month of service, he was severely wounded. He was the first American wounded in Italy during World War I. An Austrian airplane dropped a bomb near where he was on July 8, 1918. He saw a wounded soldier and dragged him to safety. One second later, a round of machine gun fire ripped through his right knee. An Italian doctor removed 28 pieces of shrapnel from his legs and bandaged his knee. Recovery would take five months.

In the hospital in Milan, Italy, Hemingway fell in love with a nurse. Her name was Agnes von Kurowsky. She was twenty-four years old, and he was nineteen. The character of Catherine Barkley

37

Europe Before World War I, 1914

The boundaries of Europe as they existed at the time of World War I. The primary powers of the war were the Allied forces of France, Great Britain, and Russia and the Central Powers of Germany and Austria-Hungary.

in Hemingway's novel *A Farewell to Arms* would be based on Nurse von Kurowsky. After Hemingway returned to Oak Park, Illinois, he soon received a letter from von Kurowsky. She was dating another lieutenant.

Hemingway went fishing in Michigan with a few friends and met a woman from Toronto, Canada, when he told his war stories at a public library. She invited him to live in her house in Toronto while she went on vacation, and he accepted.

Hemingway was soon hired as a reporter for *The Toronto Star Weekly* newspaper. He wrote exciting general interest articles such as "The Best Rainbow Trout Fishing" and "Living on $1,000 a Year in Paris." Again, his experiences as a journalist are reflected throughout his entire writing career. He returned to Illinois, this time to Chicago. At a party there, he met a beautiful young lady named Hadley Richardson. They were married on September 3, 1921.

Hemingway was then offered the position of foreign correspondent for *The Toronto Star* newspaper. This meant that the paper would pay for him to go to France, where he would write articles about what was going on in Europe and send

Ernest Hemingway needed crutches after his right knee was wounded by machine gunfire on July 8, 1918.

them to the newspaper. One of his writer friends gave him the names of other writers there, and the Hemingways set out for Paris. Like his work as a reporter in Kansas City, Ernest Hemingway's time in Paris would forever change his life.

LIFE IN PARIS

In Paris, Hemingway met Ezra Pound and Gertrude Stein. These were two American writers who gave him many writing tips. Ezra Pound was a very serious poet who revolutionized poetry by forgetting rhyme and focusing on images in as few words as possible. Gertrude Stein was a poet and novelist who focused on the sounds of words and creating a mood rather than telling a story. Hemingway often went to Stein's apartment to talk about writing and art. Her apartment was full of great paintings. They looked at the paintings, and Hemingway thought that he had to write like great painters paint. Paul Cézanne was a French painter who used simple colors and brush strokes to create wonderful paintings. Hemingway thought that he should work to write one true sentence and then another and another.

He thought he could create wonderful stories the same way Cézanne created his wonderful paintings. In a book he wrote which was not published until after his death, Ernest Hemingway discusses what to do when you do not know what to write. He told himself, "'All you have to do is write one true sentence. Write the truest sentence you know.' So finally I could write one true sentence, and then go on from there. It was easy because there was always one true sentence that I knew or had seen or had heard someone say."[4]

While Hemingway continued sending articles to *The Toronto Star,* he began writing poetry and short stories. Here is an example of his "one true sentence" idea:

> I have stood on the crowded back platform of a seven o'clock Batignolles bus as it lurched along the wet lamp lit street while men who were going home to supper never looked up from their newspapers as we passed Notre Dame grey and dripping in the rain.[5]

This is one sentence, but it tells as much as some entire stories. Readers can see the wet streets, hear the rain, smell the smells, and feel the crowded bus. Notre Dame is a famous, huge cathedral in Paris, but people are hurrying home instead of looking at the awesome cathedral. The words in Hemingway's sentence are straight-forward and clear, but the reader can easily add feeling and sense to these words.

LIFE EXPERIENCES

Ernest Hemingway had always been a strong, big person, and he became a good boxer. He prac-ticed and would fight with anyone who wanted to box. He attended many fights and met boxers and their trainers. Like all of his experiences, Hemingway's boxing knowledge would be used in his writing. Famous people he met at Gertrude Stein's apartment enjoyed talking with him about writing, art, and boxing. Hemingway seemed to know a little about everything, and he was eager to learn more and more.

The newspaper sent him to many foreign places, and Hemingway caught a serious disease called malaria on one trip. He recovered and con-tinued writing for the newspaper and for himself. In 1922, when Hemingway was on a boring assignment in Switzerland, his wife Hadley got on a train to see him. She decided to pack all of his stories and poems in a suitcase so he could work on them in Switzerland. To her horror, the suitcase was stolen at the train station in France. The contents of that suitcase would be priceless now, but the stories and poems have never been found.

Despite this huge loss, Hemingway continued to peck out news articles, stories, and poems on his typewriter. He seems to have seen himself as mainly a poet at this time. The Hemingways traveled throughout Europe, and, in Spain, Ernest Hemingway fell in love with the sport of bullfighting. In early August of 1923, Ernest Hemingway had his first book published—a thin collection titled *Three Stories and Ten Poems*. While the book was hardly read in America, having his poetry and fiction in print gave Hemingway much confidence.

Ernest and Hadley Hemingway came back to Toronto for a brief stay, and Hadley gave birth to their first child—a son they named John Hadley Nicanor Hemingway. Nicanor was the first name of a bullfighter Hemingway admired. After a few trips to Spain to participate in the famous festival (or *feria*) in Pamplona, Hemingway knew he wanted to write about Spain. He would later

Ernest and Hadley Hemingway pose for a family portrait on their wedding day in 1921.

write about his experiences at the fería in his book *The Sun Also Rises*. Hemingway even took part in a bullfight.

In addition to the lost suitcase and the birth of his son, a third thing happened to Ernest Hemingway in 1923 that changed his life. A collection of his short stories titled *in our time* was published. These stories were published again in 1925 with a few more stories and titled *In Our Time*. His book proved to the world that Ernest Hemingway was a writer to watch out for. His writing style was not like any other writer's, although many writers would later copy his style. Hemingway had established a separate kind of writing.

IN OUR TIME

Examining *In Our Time*

In Our Time consists of several short stories with very brief scenes in between them. These scenes are called vignettes or "interchapters." A vignette is a short piece of descriptive writing. Each of Hemingway's vignettes presents a scene of violence or the threat of violence. They take place in many parts of the world. Also, each has an ending that does not let the reader know exactly what will happen, a device often found in Modernism. These "open" endings are used in just about everything he wrote. Ernest Hemingway does not tell the reader what these brutal scenes mean. The reader has to think about them carefully and think about what emotions they trigger.

Think about this interchapter:

Maera lay still, his head on his arms, his face in the sand. He felt warm and sticky from the bleeding.

> Each time he felt the horn coming. Sometimes the bull only bumped him with his head. Once the horn went all the way through him and he felt it go into the sand. . . . Maera wanted to say something and he found he could not talk. Maera felt everything getting larger and larger and then smaller and smaller. Then it got larger and larger and then smaller and smaller. Then everything commenced to run faster and faster as when they speed up a cinematograph film. Then he was dead.[1]

At first a reader might think, "So what?" But a closer look reveals more about this short scene. The voice telling this story is not the bullfighter Maera, but the storyteller who knows how Maera feels and what he thinks. This could never happen in life—only in literature. Also, the writing is without emotion. Hemingway does not tell us that the goring hurts, but we can feel the hurt as we think about a horn going completely through our bodies. Also, Maera is lying face-down in the sand. He is completely powerless, extremely uncomfortable, and cannot see what is going on. He cannot speak either.

What does Maera want to say? Was he a good person? Hemingway does not answer these questions, but readers can answer them for themselves. It is possible to see a bullfight from the grandstand, and some people get to see fights from the perspective of a bullfighter. But no one knows what happens to a dying bullfighter. Hemingway imagined what it would be like, but he left room for readers to fill in their own ideas. Imagine the sound of an angry bull just inches from your face and the huge crowd screaming. Imagine your face in the sand. Imagine the shrinking and expanding, the speeding up.

Then Hemingway gets back to the storyteller's voice and tells us, "Then he was dead." What happens then? No one knows, but readers can imagine.

In Our Time contains many scenes of suffering, death, drunkenness, and dark courage. Also, the endings of the stories do not leave the reader feeling satisfied and happy. The interchapter titled "L'Envoi" involves a king talking about how he is glad a general has some soldiers shot. The king wishes another general would have had more men shot. Then Hemingway writes, "It was very jolly. We talked for a long time. Like all Greeks he wanted to go to America."[2] This is an example of irony. It is ironic because there really is nothing jolly about killing. Killing is very serious and sad. Hemingway uses irony here to show how powerful leaders can forget that war and killing are not simply parts of a game. Hemingway knew about soldiers and also about generals and world leaders. He knew the suffering that soldiers go through, and he wanted his readers to understand that, too.

This interchapter is also ironic in another way. The king of Greece cannot leave the palace grounds because he has been overthrown by revolutionary soldiers. He is giving military advice while his military leadership has fallen apart. Also, the fact that the king of Greece wants to go to America is ironic. The king should stay and rule his land. He is a bad leader.

NICK ADAMS

In his book *In Our Time*, Ernest Hemingway introduced the character Nick Adams. As Hemingway biographer James R. Mellow writes, "The invention of Nick Adams was one of the most vital inspirations of Hemingway's career."[3]

Although Nick Adams is only a character, he had many of the same experiences Hemingway had. Living in Paris and traveling throughout Europe, Ernest Hemingway had met many interesting and important people. At one time or another, he made almost all of these people mad at him by writing stories about them. Hemingway changed the people's names in the stories, but most people knew whom the embarrassing stories were about.

Because of this, Hemingway had many acquaintances but few close, true friends. He was a man alone in a crowd. He did what he thought was right, and he admitted when he was wrong. He only took someone's advice when he felt it was the right thing to do. These were Hemingway's principles. This was his code.

THE HERO AND THE CODE

Nick Adams and a few of Hemingway's other characters have been called "code heroes" by those who study literature. Nick is driven to do what he thinks is right. He is not very concerned with what others say or how other characters tell him to live. The code hero is a character who is confident in his beliefs and who trusts himself as a guide rather than let others tell him what to do. A person's code is that person's principles or morals. If a character does not break his or her

CODE HERO—
A type of Hemingway character who is confident in his beliefs and shows "grace under pressure."

code, then that character is a hero. The main male character in a book or story is called a hero. Many times, Hemingway's code hero suffers because of his code.

In the late 1930s, many Americans went to Spain to fight in the Spanish Civil War because of their code. They wanted to stop the spread of fascism. Many writers went to Spain, too, but they mainly went as writers for newspapers. The war officially began in July 1936, but the country had been growing more restless since 1931.

The character Nick Adams follows a code. Hemingway wrote about Nick Adams in many stories. Nick travels to places Hemingway traveled to, and Nick meets the people Hemingway met (although their names are changed). Nick Adams first appears in a very short story called "Did You Ever Kill Anyone?" That story takes place in World War I, and Nick is wounded much like Hemingway had been wounded.

In the story "Indian Camp," Nick and his father are in an area very much like the one Hemingway and his father went to in Michigan. In the story, as in real life, the father is a doctor.

In "Indian Camp" and a few other stories about Nick Adams when he is young, Nick is not really a code hero because he has not lived long enough to establish a code. It takes experience for a person to develop a set of morals to live by, and the young Nick is just beginning to develop his code. In these stories Nick's father is helping Nick make his code.

All the stories that feature Nick Adams show that Nick does not really fit in with the people around him. However, Nick does not seem to be troubled by that. He has a very good idea of who he is. He knows his strengths and weaknesses, and he tries to be honest and fair. In these respects he is very similar to Hemingway.

In some stories (like "Indian Camp"), Nick is a boy, and in many more stories he is a man. Hemingway considered his story "Big Two-Hearted River" to be the best one about Nick Adams. It is in *In Our Time*, and he wrote it when he was twenty-five years old.

LIVING FOR THE MOMENT

Another aspect of the Hemingway hero is his distrust in anything but the here and now. The soldiers and bullfighters in Hemingway's fiction know that they might die at any time. They also recognize that people change throughout life. What seemed certain once might seem totally different now; memory cannot be trusted. The only thing that can be trusted is the present moment.

In *For Whom the Bell Tolls*, Maria asks Robert Jordan if he loves her. He answers, "Yes, I love you now . . . thou art my woman now."[4] Jordan later thinks, "You have it now and that is all your whole life is; now. There is nothing else than now. There is neither yesterday, certainly, nor is there any tomorrow. How old must you be before you know that? There is only now."[5] These characters enjoy eating, drinking, and enjoying life because of the dark cloud of death that always hovers near.

THE SIMPLE JOYS

When Ernest Hemingway was making notes for his novel *A Farewell to Arms*, he jotted down a conversation between the main character (a lieutenant) and a priest. This is different from the version that was published in the book, but this first draft shows how this soldier appreciates things that affect his five senses rather than things that are more complex and sophisticated.

> [The Priest asks,] "You don't love anything?"
> [Lieutenant Henry answers,] "Yes, I love a lot of things."
> "What are they?"
> "I don't know. Lots of things."
> "What?"
> I thought a minute.
> "The night. The day. Food. Drink. Girls. Italy. Pictures. Places. Swimming. Portofino. Paris. Spring. Summer. Fall. Winter. Heat. Cold. Smells. Sleep. Newspapers. Reading."[6]

Portofino is a type of wine. The things the soldier likes are things that touch the five senses: sight, hearing, smell, touch, taste.

"Big Two-Hearted River"

There is very little action in "Big Two-Hearted River," but there is much to entertain the five senses. Nick hikes alone to the river, takes a nap, sets up his tent, sleeps, wakes up, eats, fishes, and goes back to his tent. The sentences in the story are short, and almost all of the words are simple.

Hemingway seems to have followed the Kansas City *Star* writing rules when he wrote this story. The reader can only guess where Nick came from and why he is there. It seems that fishing is not the main reason for Nick to go on this fishing trip. It seems like he does it to clear his head and to be alone.

Performing the jobs of setting up camp, cooking, and fishing make Nick feel good because he is in control of what he does. He can do whatever he wants to do. He pours both a can of pork and beans and a can of spaghetti into the frying pan. "I've got a right to eat this kind of stuff, if I'm willing to carry it," Nick says to himself.

This makes the reader think that Nick had previously been in some situation where he was not in control of what he could do. Because the fictional life of Nick Adams was so much like the real life of Ernest Hemingway, it may be that Nick returned injured from the war and went fishing to feel both better and more in control.

While the short story seems to go nowhere, it really tells a lot about Nick Adams. The reader has to take the evidence Hemingway gives and discover what it all means. Gertrude Stein had taught Hemingway that the writer should not tell too much; the reader uses imagination and logic to fill in any gaps in a story.

THE ICEBERG THEORY

Hemingway compared this idea to an iceberg. In a 1958 interview with writer George Plimpton, Hemingway said, "I always try to write on the principle of the iceberg. There is seven-eighths of it underwater for every part that shows." This has been called Hemingway's Iceberg Theory. He thought that writing that revealed too much was boring and not as powerful as writing that made the reader fill in the blanks.

It is fun to consider the possibilities in Hemingway's writing using the iceberg principle. The top of the iceberg is what we see on the page, what he shows us. What are the possibilities below the surface? In the famous story "Hills Like White Elephants," what is the relationship between the American and the girl? What are they going to do? Many people think they are waiting for a train to take the girl to have an abortion. This may be so, but then what? What else lies below the surface? Do they love each other? Will the American stay with her or return to America? Is this the way the characters usually treat each other?

A reader could make a list of the possibilities. Studying a story closely could eliminate some of them. This works when the reader takes what is known about a character and studies how that works with the other elements in a story.

For example, the man is called an American, and he does not speak much Spanish. Therefore, we can assume he has not been in Spain long. We know they are in Spain because the Ebro River is mentioned. The man and the girl are having a discussion, but it almost seems like they are having two different discussions at the same time. She seems to think they are making life worse, and he thinks things will be better. At the end of the story, the girl seems to be the stronger of the two because she says she will be fine. She thinks there is nothing wrong with her (possibly meaning that there is something wrong with him).

CODE CONFLICTS

The idea of a character sticking to his or her code sometimes leads to conflicts with other characters. Sticking to a code could even mean breaking a law. There is a famous scene in *A Farewell to Arms* that shows the Italian retreat at Caporetto. The army had to move back because they were being beaten by enemy forces. The scene (covering chapters 28 to 31) shows what war is really like from the soldier's perspective.

In one scene, Frederic Henry asks two soldiers to help him get the car out from the mud. The soldiers refuse, and Henry shoots one of the soldiers. This seems like a terrible thing to do, but Frederic Henry does it because those two soldiers are not doing their duty. They refused to obey Henry, and the punishment for such behavior is death. Henry does not enjoy doing this, but he has to.

SEPARATE PEACE

Maintaining a code sometimes means isolating yourself from others. Hemingway calls this a "separate peace." In *A Farewell to Arms*, Frederic Henry thinks, "I had the paper but I did not read it because I did not want to read about the war. I was going to forget the war. I had made a separate peace."[7] He has accepted his situation and found a different way to peace in wartime.

There is a one-page scene in *In Our Time* in which Nick Adams is sitting against a church wall. It is during a battle. Next to Nick is his friend Rinaldi, but Rinaldi is lying facedown, seriously injured. Nick is also injured—he was hit in the spine. He says to Rinaldi, "You and me we've made a separate peace."[8] This line looks simple, but it could be very complex. Like an iceberg, we see the simple sentence, but more is hidden below the surface, and the reader has to think about what that bigger part below might be.

Peace might mean the end of war, but Nick and Rinaldi might have found a different kind of peace. Maybe they fear they are going to die, so they prayed to God. That could be a separate peace. Or maybe they have realized that fighting is not the best solution to whatever problems both sides of the battle are having. If they decided to give up fighting, they found a separate peace that way. The war would continue, but they made peace for themselves. Or maybe they will not be able to fight in the war because of their injuries. If they cannot fight, then they made peace that way.

"THE KILLERS"

Another famous story featuring Nick Adams is "The Killers," published in 1927. Readers today might be surprised that Hemingway used the word "nigger" in the story to refer to the African-American cook. Hemingway did that because that is what people in a diner in the outskirts of Chicago would have said in the 1920s. It is important to realize the characters call the cook that, but the narrator (which also represents Hemingway's voice) calls him "the cook." The word was offensive then, but some people used it anyway. People now understand it is a hurtful word and do not use it.

Two professional killers come to the diner looking for Ole Anderson, a former professional boxer. They know he goes to the diner a lot, so they tie up the cook and Nick Adams, who is a customer, and wait for Ole Anderson. Anderson does not come to the diner, and the killers leave. Despite the danger, Nick decides to tell Anderson the killers are looking for him, but Anderson does nothing to avoid this certain death. Nick seems to be the only character who is concerned.

Boxing is a violent sport. The landlady where

Ole lives says he does not act like a boxer. "You'd never know it except from the way his face is. . . . He's just as gentle."[9] Ole Anderson's face must look like he got hit a lot. A really good boxer would not get hit that much and would probably have enough money to buy a house.

Hemingway tells us Ole Anderson was a "heavyweight prizefighter." Therefore, we can guess his last years as a boxer were not good ones. He was once a great boxer, but now he is nobody special. It seems that Ole Anderson accepts violence in life and is willing to pay the ultimate price for some mistake he made. He gives up.

Anderson feels he has to suffer for what he did, and he waits for them to kill him. Although the story is called "The Killers," it is more about how Nick Adams feels about Ole Anderson and the other characters. Nick cannot believe they do not want to try to stop the killing. The other characters have been in the town longer than Nick has, and they accept what is going on. Nick is new to the town, and he wants to leave. Nick does not want to become another person who accepts tragedy.

"INDIAN CAMP"

A younger Nick Adams appears in the story "Indian Camp," from *In Our Time*. In this story, we learn that Nick's father is a doctor, just like Hemingway's was in real life. Nick, his father, and his uncle go to a cabin where a Native American woman is about to give birth. Dr. Adams helps with the delivery as the woman's husband waits in a bunk bed over the woman. The woman is screaming because the baby will not come out. Dr. Adams has to perform an operation to help the baby out. Nick did not watch this.

When the baby is born, Nick watches his father take a blanket off the husband on the upper bunk. Nick and his father see that the man has killed himself by cutting his throat. They talk about it on the way back to their cabin. The story ends, "In the early morning on the lake sitting in the stern of the boat with his father rowing, he felt quite sure that he would never die."[10]

Just like in "The Killers," Nick Adams refuses to totally give into feeling that life is unfair. His father says the husband killed himself because "he couldn't stand things."[11] Nick thinks he is stronger than that; that he will be able to stand things. Even at his young age, Nick understands that life is unpredictable. He believes that he will never die because he thinks he is tough enough to make his life what he wants it to be.

It is interesting to compare the young Nick Adams in "Indian Camp" to the older, more experienced Nick Adams in "Big, Two-Hearted River." "Indian Camp" is the second story in *In Our Time*, and "Big, Two-Hearted River" is the last. In "Big, Two-Hearted River" Nick does not want to fish in the deep swamp because "the fishing would be tragic. In the swamp fishing was a tragic adventure. Nick did not want it."[12] This older Nick no longer feels as if he will live forever. He knows that he has to be careful.

The beauty of simple writing is that the reader can make up his or her own meaning. One reader can think it means one thing, and another reader can think it means something else. Both readers can be right.

FAME AND FORTUNE

By this time, Hemingway still wrote some poetry, but he liked writing short stories much more.

Publishers thought *In Our Time* was shocking when they first read it because of the violence and rough language in some scenes. Hemingway changed a few things, and the book was released by a larger publishing company in October 1925. Several large magazines and newspapers wrote about his book, and the interest immediately made Hemingway a famous writer.

PUBLIC REACTION

People liked how the iceberg principle worked in Hemingway's stories to make realistic characters. His writing style was compared to the painting style of famous painters like Pablo Picasso. F. Scott Fitzgerald, Gertrude Stein, *Time* magazine, *The New York Times* newspaper, and many other people and publications could tell that Hemingway was going to be a great writer. (Hemingway also became a close friend to fellow author, F. Scott Fitzgerald.)

Hemingway loved his new popularity, and he met many more important people in Paris. People who met him were impressed with his honest style, his strength, his war stories, and his knowledge of literature. Ernest and Hadley

Hemingway went to many parties and traveled throughout Europe having fun. Hemingway's tall, strong body and his confident attitude earned him the nickname "Papa." In a short time, people around the world would know who Papa was.

HOPE IN THE FUTILITY

Examining
The Sun Also Rises

As Hemingway became more and more popular, he appeared to feel more confident about writing what he thought of the world. After seeing what war was like, suffering lost love, and living the life of an American in Paris, Hemingway began to feel there was much futility in life.

Futility means uselessness or serving no purpose. Hemingway's writings all communicate that humans cannot really control what happens to them. Sometimes good people die young, and sometimes bad people live long lives. Since this is true, all people can do is enjoy life and try to be good. This is the main idea of the Lost Generation. It would also become one of the primary themes

67

FUTILITY—*The feeling of helplessness; a feeling that results cannot be predicted or expected.*

of Hemingway's classic novel, *The Sun Also Rises*. There is hope, however. After all, the sun rises as well as sets.

Return for a moment to the short story, "Cross Country Snow." In this story, Nick Adams and his friend George have a great time skiing in Switzerland. They take a break at a lodge house and talk. George may have to move back to the United States, and Nick is worried that they will not get to ski together again.

> "Maybe we'll never go skiing again, Nick," George said.
> "We've got to," said Nick. "It isn't worth while if you can't."
> "We'll go, all right," George said.
> "We've got to," Nick agreed.
> "I wish we could make a promise about it," George said.
> Nick stood up. He buckled his wind jacket tight. He leaned over George and picked up the two ski poles from against the wall. He stuck one of the ski poles into the floor.
> "There isn't any good in promising," he said.[1]

At that moment Nick does not think life is worth living if you cannot ski. He also realizes it is no use to promise they will ski together again because he has no idea what the future will bring. They can promise to ski again, but that does not mean they will be able to ski next year. You can hope to ski, but it is not certain.

They still got to ski down the rest of the mountain, though. At the end of "Cross Country Snow," Hemingway writes, "Nick put on his gloves. George was already started up the road, his skis on his shoulder. Now they would have the run home together."[2] They cannot promise to ski in the future, but now they know they will ski together. *Now* is all they can count on.

When Nick Adams sets up camp at the Big, Two-Hearted River, he remembers a friend of his named Hopkins. He was camping with Hopkins and another friend on the Black River when news came that oil was discovered on land Hopkins owned. The three friends decided that they would fish again the next year and take a yacht cruise along the north shore of Lake Superior. Then Nick realizes that he never saw Hopkins again. It was futile to make plans to go fishing and cruising. His memory of Hopkins is not sad, though. Nick still makes coffee the way Hopkins used to when they went camping. Nick laughs because the coffee turns out too bitter to drink.

Nick was afraid to fish the swamp, but he tells himself, "There were plenty of days coming when he could fish the swamp."[3] This thought, however, could prove to be futile. There is a chance he will never get to fish the swamp. Still, he likes to think that he will. That is his hope.

"NADA" MEANS NOTHING

Futility is the basis for nihilism. Nihilism is the belief that human existence is completely pointless and useless. True nihilism is the belief that God, manners, property, marriage, morality, and other things made by society have no real value. Hemingway was not a true nihilist. He very much believed in the importance of manners and morals. Some readers think he was a nihilist because of some instances in his stories where a character questions the point of life.

NIHILISM—
The belief that human existence is completely pointless and useless.

The old waiter in "A Clean, Well-Lighted Place" talks to himself as he walks home very late at night. He has a sense of fear, but he cannot figure out what it is he fears. Hemingway

Ernest, Hadley, and son John relax during a ski vacation in Schruns, Austria.

writes, "What did he fear? It was not fear or dread. It was a nothing that he knew too well. It was all a nothing and a man was nothing too."[4] The old waiter thinks a clean, well-lighted place where a person can be treated with respect is very important. The young waiter cannot understand this. The old waiter values dignity very highly, but the young waiter cannot see the dignity in people. Dignity and respect are the only things that matter to the old waiter. He developed this attitude from his life experiences, but he is not a true nihilist. He values the happiness of others over his own happiness.

Another part of "A Clean, Well-Lighted Place" that confuses many readers is what the old waiter thinks next on his way home. He thinks of prayers, but he changes the words to suit his mood:

> Some lived in it and never felt it [a feeling of emptiness] but he knew it all was *nada y pues nada y nada y pues nada*. Our *nada* who art in *nada, nada* be thy name thy kingdom *nada* thy will be *nada* in *nada* as it is in *nada*. Give us this *nada* out daily *nada* and *nada* us our *nada* as we *nada* our *nadas*.[5]

The old waiter feels that even prayers mean nothing. He probably learned the prayers growing up, but the religion of his youth is not working for the older man. He carries some Christian values (like helping those in need and treating people fairly), but he thinks the prayers are worthless. The old waiter's principles are misunderstood, and he feels like a stranger.

FIESTA

Hadley and Ernest Hemingway vacationed in Spain for the third time in the summer of 1925. They went to bullfights and spent many nights drinking Spanish wine. They stayed all summer, and Ernest jotted down in notebooks interesting words or sentences he heard. He knew from the start how he wanted to write about their experiences in Spain. He had some success with his early short stories, but he wanted to write a novel. In a novel, he could tell one long story and also slip in smaller stories. He could also write more about the characters.

He started typing the novel while on vacation in Northern Spain. Then he and Hadley went to a resort town in France, where he continued writing in notebooks. In one month, Ernest Hemingway had written over 250 notebook pages, and he finished writing his novel *Fiesta* in Paris on September 21, 1925. The entire book is about his experiences with friends in the city of Pamplona, in Northern Spain. He changed the names of the characters, but it is easy to figure out which of his friends is a character in the book.

He did not like the title *Fiesta*, and he thought of changing it to *The Lost Generation* because of the story about Gertrude Stein and the mechanic. He finally chose to name his first novel *The Sun Also Rises*. He chose that title from the Bible—Ecclesiastes, Chapter 1, Verses 4–5, which reads:

> One generation passeth away, and another generation cometh: but the earth abideth for ever. The sun ariseth, and the sun goeth down, and hasteth to his place where he arose.

The message of the book of Ecclesiastes is that life should be enjoyed but also that things can happen that no one can control. The smartest person can seem like a fool compared to the power of nature. William Shakespeare also used the ideas in Ecclesiastes in a few of his famous plays. Ecclesiastes is very much about the futility of humans.

This futility is evident in *The Sun Also Rises*.

Robert Cohn was a boxing champion in college, but he hates boxing. He really wants to be a writer. The character who tells the story, Jake Barnes, had an injury in that war that left him impotent. Jake and Lady Brett Ashley seem to be in love with each other, but they can never really be with each other because of Jake's injury and because Brett is already married. Another of the friends in the novel, Michael Campbell, is in love with Brett. Brett likes a bullfighter named Romero, but she eventually decides to marry Michael once she's divorced her husband.

LOST AND UNHAPPY

Each of these characters wants something he or she cannot get. No matter how hard they try, they cannot find meaning in their lives. In fact, at the end of the novel, none of the characters have really changed. Many people think the Lost Generation were bad people because they drank too much alcohol, wasted money, and spent too much time at parties instead of at work.

A popular idea about the Lost Generation is that many people felt the War was useless and another sign that people cannot control their destinies. They thought that they might as well have a good time since they could not control the future. The writer F. Scott Fitzgerald wrote about this idea in his book *Tender is the Night*. In Fitzgerald's book and in *The Sun Also Rises*, characters who live this party life feel lost and unhappy.

THE DESIGN OF THE NOVEL

Ernest Hemingway asked a few of his friends for advice on the book as he wrote it. F. Scott Fitzgerald suggested a different beginning, and Hemingway took his advice and changed it. Authors almost never write anything in one shot; they go back and go back, changing and fixing things many times before they think it is good enough to publish.

The Sun Also Rises is divided into three books. The first book introduces Cohn, Brett, and Jake. They are in Paris, all unhappy. What carries this first book is the realistic dialogue. Hemingway reveals much about the characters through dialogue.

Robert Cohn tells Jake Barnes he is sick of

Paris, and he wants to do something else. Jake begins the dialogue:

> "I've had plenty to worry about one time or other. I'm through worrying."
> "Well, I want to go to South America."
> "Listen, Robert, going to another country doesn't make any difference. I've tried all that. You can't get away from yourself by moving from one place to another. There's nothing to that."[6]

WORDS AND ACTIONS

The interesting thing about this little bit of dialogue is that it reveals that Jake has been through a bad experience. We learn that he is from Kansas City, so the fact that he is in Paris means that he, himself, has tried going to another country. This is what he tells Cohn not to do. Jake believes that the only way to escape problems is to change the way you think. He says he has stopped worrying, but he has plenty of worries. That very night he cannot sleep.

> I lay awake thinking and my mind jumping around. Then I couldn't keep away from it [the war experiences], and I started to think about Brett and all the rest of it went away. I was thinking about Brett and my mind stopped jumping

77

around and started to go in sort of smooth waves. Then all of a sudden I started to cry. Then after a while it was better and I lay in bed and listened to the heavy trams go by and way down the street, and then I went to sleep."[7]

Just as moving to another place is no way to escape problems, merely saying you are "through with worrying" does not mean you do not have worries. The only thing that matters is action. Talking about something is useless; you have to do it. This is another idea from the Lost Generation. This is what Brett is talking about when she says, "Let's not talk. Talking's all bilge."[8] Bilge means worthless junk. Nick Adams would agree with Brett. That is why he did not promise to go skiing again with George in "Cross Country Snow."

A DARK ENDING

The mood or feeling of the ending of *The Sun Also Rises* is much like that of a short story by F. Scott Fitzgerald called "Babylon Revisited." Hemingway thought this was a great story. In Fitzgerald's story, a man locks his wife out of their house one cold winter night because they are both drunk and he thinks she is interested in another man.

The woman eventually dies from an illness she got from that cold night. Their only child is sent to live with the woman's sister. The man comes back after a couple of years to try to convince his sister-in-law to let him have his daughter back. He has her almost convinced, but a couple of old party friends of his show up and remind the sister-in-law of his drunken past. He does not get custody of his daughter.

The Sun Also Rises is different because we do not know what will happen in the future after Brett and Jake part ways. The reader can assume, however, that there will not be a very happy ending. Bret says she will be nice to Mike, but she has made promises before that she did not keep.

The Sun Also Rises ends with Jake and Brett in the back of a taxi. They are going for a ride before Brett returns to Mike. "Oh, Jake," Brett says, "we could have had such a damned good time together." Jake answers, "Isn't it pretty to think so?"[9] This is yet another example of Hemingway's notion of hope within futility.

Both Brett and Jake know they probably never would have had a good time together because of the kind of people they are. Although Jake may appear to be agreeing that the two of them could have been happy together in different circumstances, it seems doubtful that he really believes this. Or perhaps he is merely recognizing how pointless it is to speculate about what might have been.

A New Love

Immediately after finishing *The Sun Also Rises*, Ernest Hemingway wrote a few more excellent short stories and began writing another novel. This new book was a parody. A parody is humorous writing that makes fun of another book. The book Hemingway was making fun of was *Dark Laughter* by Sherwood Anderson. Hemingway titled it *The Torrents of Spring*. Many of Hemingway's friends thought it was mean to make fun of another writer. Sherwood Anderson said he disliked *The Torrents of Spring*, but he did not mind if Hemingway published it. It was published.

Pauline Pfeiffer, a friend of Hadley, thought the book was very funny. She was an editor for *Vogue* magazine. Hemingway eventually fell in love with Pfeiffer. Hadley Hemingway knew that Ernest loved Pauline, so she said she would grant

PARODY—*A work in which one writer imitates and exaggerates another writer's work.*

80

Ernest Hemingway and Pauline Pfeiffer, shortly
before they were wed in 1927.

him a divorce if he and Pauline still loved each other after being separated for 100 days. As a result, Hemingway spent much of the year traveling in 1926. F. Scott Fitzgerald helped him polish *The Sun Also Rises* during this time.

By the end of the 100 days, Pauline and Ernest did still love each other, and Ernest and Hadley were legally separated. Soon afterward, *The Sun Also Rises* was published. Hemingway dedicated the novel to his wife and son: "This book is for Hadley and for John Hadley Nicanor."

The Sun Also Rises earned Hemingway much money and fame. He traveled with Pauline to Key West, Florida, meeting famous artists along the way. He fished almost every day in Key West. Memories of his fishing adventures later became key parts of another novel. On May 10, 1927, Hemingway and Pauline were married.

A curious accident happened to Ernest Hemingway in March 1928. He came home after having dinner with some friends, and he went into the bathroom. Toilets in France used to (and many still do) flush by pulling a cord. Hemingway reached for the flushing cord but instead pulled a cord leading to a ceiling skylight. The glass window fell on his head, and the scar left on his forehead is visible in many photographs of him.

Patrick Hemingway was born in the summer of 1928, and Hemingway was already several hundred pages into writing another novel. This one was to be called *A Farewell to Arms*.

To War

Examining "Francis Macomber" and *A Farewell to Arms*

Back in 1925, Ernest Hemingway wrote in a letter to writer F. Scott Fitzgerald that "war is the best subject of all. It groups the maximum of material and speeds up the action and brings out all sorts of stuff that normally you have to wait a lifetime to get."[1] Hemingway's experiences in World War I provided the information for *A Farewell to Arms*. With his sister Sunny typing for him six hours a day for five weeks, the novel was finished in January 1929.

The sadness Ernest Hemingway felt when his father Clarence committed suicide was lessened a little when he was offered a large amount of money for *A Farewell to Arms*. He carefully checked over his writing and rewrote most of it before sending it to the publisher. The publisher thought Hemingway used too much bad language in the book, and Max Perkins, the editor, convinced Hemingway to change or hide the profanity. The novel quickly became a bestseller.

Ernest Hemingway got the title of this book from a poem by George Peele, a writer in the late 1500s. Peele's poem was dedicated to Queen Elizabeth I. It is about an old man who was once a brave soldier. His battle helmet became a home for bees, and his blonde hair became gray. His devotion to the queen, however, remained as strong as ever.

A Farewell to Arms ends without the reader knowing what will happen next to the soldier. Considering the poem, though, the reader might guess that the soldier will continue to fight for what he thinks is right. He will not simply give up, which would be the easy thing to do in his circumstances.

A Farewell to Arms is based on many of Hemingway's own experiences during World War I in Italy. The hero of the novel, Frederic Henry, is an American ambulance driver. He suffers an injury very similar to Hemingway's real-life war injury and falls in love with a nurse in an Italian hospital. In this novel, Hemingway uses the same kind of dialogue that made *The Sun Also Rises* such an excellent book, and he adds

Hemingway and his hospital nurse, Agnes von Kurowsky. Von Kurowsky would later serve as the inspiration for Catherine Barkley in *A Farewell to Arms*.

other details to make his characters seem perfectly real. James R. Mellow writes, "Each of these characters is well defined, crackling with life."[2]

When readers know a lot about a character, they begin to care about what happens to that character. In *A Farewell to Arms*, we care about Frederic Henry and many other characters, too. Hemingway uses his iceberg principle to give these other details deep meaning. For example, here is a passage from the short first chapter:

> Troops went by the house and down the road and the dust they raised powdered the leaves of the trees. The trunks of the trees too were dusty and the leaves fell early that year and we saw the troops marching along the road and the dust rising and leaves, stirred by the breeze, falling and the soldiers marching and afterward the road bare and white except for the leaves.[3]

This passage tells us a lot about how the person telling the story feels about what is going on. The dust raised by the soldiers marching by covers everything, and the leaves fell early that year. This means that it is not natural. The dust is rising, and the leaves are falling. The soldiers are marching down the road, and then they are gone. There is much motion in these two sentences. Also, the second sentence is very long.

Hemingway did this to connect the marching troops to the early falling leaves and to give the feeling of a long line of soldiers as they march along. Therefore, what seems like nothing more than soldiers marching along means much more. It sets the feeling for the whole novel.

> There were mists over the river and clouds on the mountain and the trucks splashed mud on the road and the troops were muddy and wet in their capes; their rifles were wet under their capes and the two leather cartridge-boxes on the front of their belts, grey leather boxes heavy with the packs of clips of thin, long 6.5 mm. cartridges, bulged forward under the capes so that the men, passing on the road, marched as though they were six months gone with child.[4]

"Gone with child" means pregnant. Hemingway creates a wicked image the careful reader can pick up. Instead of the beauty and joy of a woman being pregnant, Hemingway gives us muddy soldiers carrying weapons into war. Instead of a baby, the soldiers are carrying things to kill people. Instead of a nice sunny picture, Hemingway paints a misty, muddy, and dark picture. The tip of this iceberg hints at the tragedy and destruction that lies below the surface.

In the middle of the novel, Frederic Henry

says, "I was always embarrassed by the words sacred, glorious, and sacrifice and the expression in vain."[5]

This is the same idea as Brett Ashley saying that talk is worthless. Hemingway felt that certain words are used incorrectly so much that they have lost their real meaning. This idea runs throughout all of Ernest Hemingway's writing.

A TRAGIC END

The tragic ending of *A Farewell to Arms* leaves the reader certain that war is terrible. It also makes us feel the futility of modern life. The nurse Frederic Henry falls in love with, Catherine Barkley, is a person who tries to do good. However, in the end, she is not rewarded for her good deeds. Frederic Henry's prayers go unanswered, and he wonders why Catherine is suffering instead of him. The novel is both soft and rough, nice and cruel, sweet and bitter. And this is how Hemingway felt about war.

This novel was another huge success, and Hemingway began writing a book about bullfighting. He also went hunting and relaxed.

Throughout his adult life, Ernest Hemingway suffered many accidents. He had a badly cut eye, the disease anthrax, a large gash on his forehead (which, as mentioned, are visible in many photographs of him), a badly broken arm, blown-up knees, a severely cut leg and finger, and a ripped chin. But he was generally healthy and remained active, so these injuries did not slow him down.

Pauline's uncle Gus bought a house in Key West, Florida, as a gift to Pauline and Ernest. Before relocating there, the Hemingways went to Kansas City so Pauline could have a baby. Gregory Hancock Hemingway was born on November 12, 1931.

Hemingway finished his book on bullfighting and titled it *Death in the Afternoon*. The book was not immediately liked by many reviewers, but it is still one of the most informative books on bullfighting.

In 1933, Ernest Hemingway went to Africa. As usual, his experiences were later made into stories. The most famous stories from his African experiences are "The Short Happy Life of Francis Macomber," "The Snows of Kilimanjaro," and the novel *Green Hills of Africa*. He was happiest when he was writing.

FRANCIS MACOMBER

"The Short Happy Life of Francis Macomber" is one of Hemingway's best-known stories. Written in 1936, it is a tale of fear, codes, and justice. In the story, a wealthy American couple, the Macombers, hire a professional hunter to help them on a hunt in Africa. Francis Macomber ends up acting like a coward when he runs from a wounded lion.

The professional hunter, Robert Wilson, is a handsome, strong man. Macomber's wife makes fun of her cowardly husband to Wilson, and she even offers herself romantically to Wilson that night. The whole safari is uncomfortable because of the cowardice of Francis Macomber, the embarrassment of his wife, and the rugged good looks of Wilson. Wilson also breaks his code as a hunter when he allows Mr. Macomber to chase game in the car.

To make up for his cowardly fleeing, Francis Macomber goes in the bush to kill a wounded bull buffalo. After that earlier embarrassing

Ernest and Pauline pose before the day's catches
with sons Patrick, Gregory, and John ("Bumby").

moment, he now feels brave. "As the car moved slowly across the open space toward the island of bushy trees that ran in a tongue of foliage along a dry water course that cut the open swale, Macomber felt his heart pounding and his mouth was dry again, but it was excitement, not fear."[6]

The gun bearer says the bull buffalo is dead, but it comes charging out of the bush. Wilson and Macomber take a few shots at the furious beast. Mrs. Macomber, who was a ways off watching the incident, took a shot, too. Her shot did not hit the buffalo. It hit and killed her husband.

The question readers must ask themselves is this: Did Margot Macomber aim to kill the buffalo or her husband? If she did intend to shoot her husband, did she do it because he was a coward or because she was afraid of his new courage? Did she shoot at the charging bull buffalo to save her husband or Wilson? Maybe she is braver than her husband is. Maybe she wanted to save Wilson in order to further a relationship with him.

If she intended to shoot Robert Wilson, did she do it because she wanted to start a fresh relationship with her husband? After all, Wilson did duck right before Mrs. Macomber's shot. She also made the shot from the car, something she earlier noted was unfair and wrong.

The last page of the story reveals what Wilson and Mrs. Macomber say they believe. Is what they say the truth? In order to answer this question, we have to consider how Mrs. Macomber felt about her husband. Compared to the great hunter Wilson, Francis Macomber seems like a weak man. Although they had been married for eleven years, at the beginning of the story Margot Macomber looked at both her husband and Wilson "as though she had never seen them before."[7]

Since it is as if she had never seen them before, we can forget the history Francis and Margot Macomber have. Now we can compare Robert Wilson to Francis Macomber. Wilson had "extremely cold blue eyes with faint white wrinkles at the corners that grooved merrily when he smiled." He had large shotgun shells in his belt, and Mrs. Macomber noticed "his big brown hands, his old slacks, his very dirty boots."[8] Wilson was a real man, not just someone who wore manly clothes and pretended to be a real man.

Francis is described as being "very well built if you did not mind that length of bone, dark, his hair cropped like an oarsman, rather thin-lipped, and was considered handsome. He was dressed in the same sort of safari clothes that Wilson wore except that his were new, . . . and he had just shown himself, very publicly, to be a coward."[9]

Macomber dresses like a real man, but his manliness does not seem to go beyond his clothing. His wife makes it clear she respects real men, and she works to make her husband seem even weaker. Hemingway writes that women like Margot Macomber are "predatory."[10] This means that they live by destroying others. In this sense, Mrs. Macomber and Robert Wilson are the same; they are both predators. Mrs. Macomber lives by destroying her husband, and Mr. Wilson lives by destroying wild animals.

"MACOMBER" AND CODES

One aspect of "The Short Happy Life of Francis Macomber" is codes and code breaking. The story shows the strict rules of big game hunting and the code of the bush. Wilson breaks a few rules: he allows game chasing from the car and he lashes the natives instead of making them pay fines. Wilson thinks that his standards (his code) could change if his clients had different standards.

> Their standards were his standards as long as they were hiring him.
>
> They were his standards in all except the shooting. He had his own standards about the killing and they could live up to them or get some one else to hunt them. He knew, too, that they all respected him for this.[11]

So maybe Robert Wilson does have a code that he does not break. There are instances in Hemingway's fiction where a person's code and the code of law conflict. There are times when a character breaks a law because he has to in order to keep from breaking his own code. Wilson does not care about stealing another man's wife or allowing Macomber to chase game in a car. He did not break his code about not allowing an animal to suffer more than it has to and he never talks about other people who have hired him because he is a professional hunter.

Hemingway based "The Short Happy Life of

Hemingway's boat, the *Pilar*, in Key West, Florida.

Francis Macomber" on people he met on his hunting expeditions, although the shooting of Francis Macomber never happened in real life. Ernest Hemingway seemed to have a mind built for writing. He would see and experience something. Then he would think about it and the possible connections and outcomes. Then he would put his ideas into words. His stories are based on reality, but they are still fiction.

RETURN TO WAR

Ernest Hemingway bought a fine fishing boat he named *The Pilar* to dock at his Key West home. Off the coast of Key West, he once caught a 514-pound tuna. This, too, he would later write about. He also met a woman from St. Louis named Martha Gellhorn. She was a journalist, and she began to spend more and more time with Ernest and Pauline. Hemingway was thirty-eight years old, and he wanted some excitement. He got news that his favorite places in Northern Spain were being overtaken in a civil war.

The Spanish Civil War began in July 1936. The Nationalists, with help from Nazi Germany and Fascist Italy, were battling the Loyalists.

General Francisco Franco (above) became dictator of Spain in 1939 after leading the rebel Nationalist Army to victory over Loyalist forces in the Spanish Civil War.

Hemingway was strongly against Nazism and Fascism, and he took an interest in the loyalist side. He traveled to Spain in March of 1937. Throughout his entire life, Ernest Hemingway read almost constantly. His life of reading and what he experienced in Spain would provide material for his next huge success.

He went to Spain to join his friend John dos Passos and Dutch filmmaker Joris Ivens to make a film about conditions in Spain (*The Spanish Earth*) as well as write newspaper articles. Martha Gellhorn also went there, and she and Ernest sadly watched Loyalist forces being over-taken. Pauline, back in Paris, knew she was losing Ernest to Martha. They eventually divorced in December 1939.

In February 1939 he made a trip to Cuba and began writing another novel. Within three weeks, he had written 15,000 words.[12] He and Martha began renting a large but run-down house near Havana, Cuba. Hemingway eventually bought the house as a Christmas gift to himself in 1940. This house, called *Finca Vigia* (Spanish for "lookout farm"), would be the place Ernest Hemingway would engage in some of his finest writing.

He finished the new novel in August, and he thought it was the best book he had yet written. He titled it *For Whom the Bell Tolls*.

"No Man Is an Island"

For Whom the Bell Tolls is an interesting, difficult, and excellent book. It balances war with romance and shows how war affects real people. The title of the novel comes from a book by John Donne, an English poet who lived 400 years ago. In Donne's book titled *Devotions Upon Emergent Occasions*, Donne writes:

> No man is an Iland, intire of it selfe; every man is a peece of the Continent, a part of the maine . . . any mans death diminishes me, because I am involved in Mankinde; And therefore never send to know for whom the bell tolls; It tolls for thee.[13]

Donne means that all people are connected, and one person cannot live completely alone. In the old days, church bells would ring when a person was buried. Donne felt his connection to other people so strongly that he did not need to know whom the bell was ringing for. When anyone died, he felt a piece of himself dying.

This is how Robert Jordan, the hero of *For*

Whom the Bell Tolls feels, too. Jordan is an American fighting on the Loyalist side on the Spanish Civil War. He is assigned to stay with unofficial fighters living in a cave on a hillside. His goal is to blow up an important bridge. The story of the 471-page novel takes place over only 70 hours, but what happens during that time will permanently change Robert Jordan forever.

Jordan falls in love with a young Spanish woman named Maria. Maria was abused by the people the Loyalists are fighting. When they are together, they try to forget about the war, but it is impossible. Along with a few other soldiers, a woman named Pilar and her husband Pablo live in the cave. Robert Jordan thinks Pablo is a drunk, stupid man, but Pilar tells Jordan a story of how Pablo showed his bravery in battle. Pilar trembles when thinking of the story because it seems that Pablo finds pleasure in killing. The story is about 100 pages into the novel, and it is brutal enough to give readers nightmares.

Hemingway included this story to show how war is more than dots on a chart or numbers of casualties. War means children losing their parents, painful injuries, and people doing things they may later regret.

The entrance to *Finca Vigia*, Hemingway's home in Cuba.

A Circular Story

As Robert Jordan tries to carry out his mission, his love for Maria and the foolishness of Pablo and other hill fighters almost ruin his plans. Compare the first and last sentences of *For Whom the Bell Tolls*. First sentence: "He lay flat on the brown, pine-needled floor of the forest, his chin on his folded arms, and high overhead the wind blew in the tops of the pine trees." Last sentence: "He could feel his heart beating against the pine needle floor of the forest."

The setting is the same. However, very much has happened to Robert Jordan and other characters in the novel. By making the ending so much like the beginning, Hemingway makes the story seem like a circle. It seems as though this thing has happened before and that it will happen again. This is another clever trick Hemingway uses. He wrote this novel so readers would really care what happens to Jordan and Maria, but he also wrote it to be more open. The story is about Jordan and Maria, but it could be about people in other wars in other parts of the world at other times in history.

Reality in Fiction

Real-life history plays an important role in *For Whom the Bell Tolls*. Hemingway writes about the real Spanish Civil War, but he makes up characters. Some generals and soldiers in the novel are based on real people, but other characters are created from his imagination. Again, the characters he creates show how war is much more than maps and numbers. War can tear apart families and kill good people.

The first person Robert Jordan meets by the gypsy cave is an old man named Anselmo. Although he admits he has killed enemy soldiers in battle, Anselmo thinks killing a person is very bad. When Jordan asks Anselmo if he has ever killed anyone, Anselmo answers, "Yes. Several times. But not with pleasure. To me it is a sin to kill a man. Even the Fascists whom we must kill. . . . I am against the killing of men."[14]

Late in the book, Anselmo gets killed, and Jordan feels very bad about his death. Even in the confusion and noise of battle, Jordan feels sadness at Anselmo's death. Jordan knows that he, himself, is part of this terrible war although he hates it. The mission of blowing up the bridge is very important to Robert Jordan, but the lives of Maria and the others on the hillside become very important, also. Like other code heroes, Robert Jordan is more concerned with others' safety than with his own safety. In the intense, dramatic conclusion of the novel, Jordan thinks, "Each one does what he can. You can do nothing for yourself but perhaps you can do something for another."[15]

The dialogue in *For Whom the Bell Tolls* confuses many readers because it has a lot of old fashioned words like "thee" and "whom." For example, the gypsy Anselmo says to Pablo, "Until now thou hadst horses thou wert with us."[16] In more modern English, Anselmo means, "Until you had horses you were with us." Hemingway wrote it this way for two reasons. First, the characters would have spoken Spanish. The actual translations of many Spanish words are these old sounding words. In Spanish, there are ways to refer to someone you do not know very well and ways to refer to a close friend. These characters are using the first, more formal way, and that is translated into English as "thee," "thou," and so on.

The second reason is to give the book a more

classic sound. Hemingway used the old style of the John Donne quote ("It tolls for thee") throughout the entire book. Bridging the formal sounding words to the down-to-earth parts helps the reader understand the bigger picture while feeling the personal effects of the civil war. The struggle Pilar, Pablo, Maria, and the others are facing is a classic struggle of individuals against aggressive political leaders.

Throughout the novel Robert Jordan is torn between his duty and his love for Maria. When he is alone with Maria, Jordan tries as hard as he can not to think about the war. But when he is busy preparing to blow up the bridge, Jordan forces himself not to think about Maria. After Jordan shoots an enemy scout, he feels Maria next to him. Hemingway writes, "She had no place in his life now."[17]

Despite their efforts, the Loyalists in the Spanish Civil War were overpowered. *For Whom the Bell Tolls* ends with Robert Jordan in a very interesting position. It is certainly not the kind of ending found in most novels from before Hemingway's time. Readers have to figure out if it is a happy ending or if things turn out like they should. Maybe life is futile, and the only way to

Ernest Hemingway is pictured here around 1940, shortly after the publication of *For Whom the Bell Tolls*.

happiness is to try to be a good person and to not expect fair treatment.

It is important to keep in mind that *For Whom the Bell Tolls* is a mature book. Hemingway meant for it to be read by adults, and it has a few adult themes. It is also a long book. Hemingway wrote the novel when he was forty years old, and he had experienced much in those forty years.

The brilliance of *For Whom the Bell Tolls* is that it seems like more than just a story about war and love between two people. It is a story about how people treat each other and what life is all about. Robert Jordan does not have to risk his life fighting in Spain but he does it to help people who need his help. He eventually does much, much more than his duty calls for. He realizes that people are connected; it does not matter where a person is from or how they live, as long as they try to be good people.

Jordan thinks, "I suppose it is possible to live as full a life in seventy hours as in seventy years; granted that your life has been full up to the time that the seventy hours start and that you have reached a certain age."[18]

After this sentence, he thinks about what love means. Then he thinks about how terrible war is.

The way the novel shifts from dialogue to Robert Jordan's thoughts confuses some readers because Jordan is not the teller of the story but a character in it. However, many readers like the way we can see the scenes and also see into Jordan's thoughts.

For Whom the Bell Tolls was selected to receive the Pulitzer Prize for Fiction in 1941. The Pulitzer Prize is an important award for the best work of the year, that has been given every year since 1918. The Chairman of the Board, however, said the novel could not win the prize because it had a few scenes he considered profane, and he vetoed the selection of Hemingway's book.[19] There was no Pulitzer Prize for fiction for 1941.

DESTROYED BUT NOT DEFEATED

Examining *The Old Man and the Sea*

By 1941, World War II was a terrible reality in Europe. Martha Hemingway longed for adventure and set out to Europe to write about the War. Ernest stayed in Cuba spending his days fishing. It angered Martha that Ernest was not more interested in the largest war in history, and their marriage was stressed. When Hemingway went to London to meet up with his wife, he also met a journalist named Mary Welsh. She was very pretty, and Hemingway was immediately attracted to her.

Ernest Hemingway managed to be present at the Allied landing at Omaha Beach on the coast of England on D-Day (June 6, 1944). He did this less that two weeks after being in a serious car accident. Although he was only supposed to observe and write about war events for *Collier's* magazine, Ernest Hemingway saw some real battle action. He bragged about his adventures to Mary Welsh, with whom he eventually fell in love. He divorced Martha right before Christmas 1945, and he married Mary Welsh the following March.

ACROSS THE RIVER AND INTO THE TREES

In 1949, Hemingway traveled from his house in Cuba to the place in Italy where he had been seriously injured over thirty years earlier. This was a moving visit for him, and back in Cuba he wrote about how he felt as an older man returning to the spot where he felt he became a man. He titled this new novel *Across the River and into the Trees*, and it was published in September 1950. The novel is about a fifty-year-old military colonel who returns to Venice to spend time with a nineteen-year-old girl he has loved for some time. This time, combat is not the featured event, as it had been in *For Whom the Bell Tolls*.

Across the River and into the Trees was not well

received by critics, but Hemingway liked it. As in "A Clean, Well-Lighted Place," this novel centers on an older man whose dignity is still intact. His rough life is catching up to him, and he realizes he is not the strong man he once was. However, Colonel Cantwell is proud of his military service, and he does not care what people might think about him dating a girl so much younger than he is.

Colonel Cantwell was a military hero much like the real-life Andrew Jackson. General Jackson is known for his bravery in the Battle of New Orleans. He also served two terms as President of the United States. *In Across the River and into the Trees*, Hemingway writes that Jackson's last words were that he and his soldiers should go "across the river and into the trees" to rest. These are some of Colonel Cantwell's dying words, too. The comparison between Jackson and Cantwell is another example of how Hemingway's knowledge of history entered his writing.

After Christmas 1950, Ernest Hemingway began writing the story of a Cuban fisherman, and the story was finished by the end of February 1951. It was considered too short to publish as a

Ernest and Martha Hemingway at *Finca Vigia* with son Gregory and Martha's mother.

novel by itself, so *Life* magazine published it in a special edition titled *The Old Man and the Sea*, and it was an immediate, huge hit.

Santiago and "Derecho"

The Old Man and the Sea is another example of Hemingway's iceberg theory. The basic story is simple: an old fisherman goes a long time without catching any fish. Then he catches a large marlin far out at sea, and sharks eat the huge fish as he hauls it back to port. There is much more to this story, however. Santiago, the fisherman, and his catch are an allegory of a bigger story.

An allegory is a simple story with deeper meanings. For example, many see Santiago and his struggle with the huge fish to be about how people can suffer big disappointments without totally giving up. The fish could represent anything that a person struggles for.

ALLEGORY—*A writing device in which a person, object, or event has more than one meaning.*

Sometimes, students are faced with two options on a test in school. They could study hard and hope they get a good score, or they could not study at all and cheat. The cheaters might end up with a higher score on the test, but those who studied can feel better about themselves. Santiago is like those who studied for the test. While the younger fishermen made fun of him, Santiago did not let himself get angry. Also, he loved Manolin like a son, but never forgot the boy had his own parents.

About Santiago, Hemingway writes, "He was too simple to wonder when he had attained humility. But he knew he had attained it and he knew it was not disgraceful and it carried no loss of true pride."[1] This means that Santiago knew he was humble, but he knew it was real and not fake humbleness. He thinks that being honest and true to what you believe is what makes a man. Although Manolin is young, Santiago tells him "You are already a man."[2] He says this because Manolin helps him, and he seems not to care about himself.

Quite often, people do eventually get what they want, but it is not exactly as good as they thought it would be. All humans end up dying; it is how one lives that makes the difference. This idea appears in a short story titled "The Death of Ivan Ilyich" by Count Leo Tolstoy. Hemingway thought Tolstoy was an excellent writer, even

LEO TOLSTOY (1828–1910)

Russian writer Leo Tolstoy (sometimes spelled "Tolstoi") was one of the greatest novelists in the history of world literature. He was also an important philosophical thinker and social reformer.

Born into a privileged background, Tolstoy grew restless and strangely dissatisfied as a young man, and decided to join the Russian Army. Although he distinguished himself as a soldier during the Crimean War (1853–1856), he came to view war as ugly and senseless. In 1869, he released the first of his great masterpieces, *War and Peace*. A work of Russian realism, the novel rejected the "Great Man" theory of history, suggesting instead that supposedly "great" and famous individuals actually have no significant impact on the course of history.

Tolstoy's second masterpiece, the tragic love story *Anna Karenina*, was published in installments from 1875 to 1877. The novel deals with the open infidelity of a Russian princess, addressing many moral and philosophical issues faced by Russian aristocracy in the 1870s.

From 1878 to 1885, Tolstoy stopped producing fiction and instead wrote on religious and social topics. In an effort to live up to his newfound religious beliefs, Tolstoy gave up all of his property. Tolstoy even began dressing as a peasant and often worked in the fields.

Tolstoy returned to fiction with *The Death of Ivan Ilyich* (1886), a dark novella dealing with the empty and ultimately meaningless nature of life. Tolstoy also wrote several plays, including *The Power of Darkness* (1888), as well as several short stories, including "The Devil" (1889), and "The Kreutzer Sonata" (1891).

though Tolstoy wrote about fifty years before Hemingway was born. How well a writer writes is more important then when he or she writes. Ernest Hemingway did not use the phrase the Lost Generation to refer to himself because he felt he was writing about more than how one generation lived. People of all generations feel lost at some point. Similarly, *The Old Man and the Sea* is a story about anyone in any time.

RIGHT AND WRONG

In a short story called "The Butterfly and the Tank," a man comes into a bar in Spain crowded with soldiers and shoots a waiter with a water gun (called a "flit gun" in the story). Hemingway writes:

> Everybody laughed except the waiter who was carrying a tray full of drinks at the time. He was indignant.
>
> *"No hay derecho,"* the waiter said. This means, "You have no right to do that," and this is the simplest and strongest protest in Spain.
>
> [The man shoots another waiter with his water gun.]
>
> *"No hay derecho,"* he said with dignity.
>
> [The man shoots another waiter with his water gun.]

"No hay derecho," he said. This time it was no protest. It was an indictment and I saw three men in uniform start from a table for the flit gun man and the next thing all four of them were going out the revolving door in a rush and you heard a smack when someone hit the flit gun man on the mouth.[3]

Doing something you have no right to do is a very bad thing in this Spanish bar, and it is a bad thing in *The Old Man and the Sea*. The flit gun man is not just hit in the mouth but also shot and killed. He did not have a respectable code. "Indignant" means being angry at something that is unfair. An "indictment" is a strong disapproval. The flit gun man did something that was unfair, and he suffered the ultimate price for it. Santiago does what is right and dignified, and he feels good about himself for it.

This idea of right and wrong appears in much of Hemingway's writing. A character does not have respect for a general just because he is a general. A character respects only those people who are honest and fair. These people who are respected might be generals or they might be streetwalkers (as in "The Light of the World") or weak old men (as in "Old Man at the Bridge"). Of course, different people have different ideas of right and wrong. To Hemingway, dignity meant doing what you think is right. Also, he believed people should not work to hurt those they think do wrong.

About *The Old Man and the Sea*, the famous American writer William Faulkner wrote,

> Time may show it to be the best single piece of any of us. I mean his and my contemporaries. This time, he discovered God, a Creator. Until now, his men and women had made themselves, shaped themselves out of their own clay; their victories and defeats were at the hands of each other, just to prove to themselves or one another how tough they could be. But this time, he wrote about pity; about something somewhere that made them all: the old man who had to catch the fish and then lose it, the fish that had to be caught and then lost, the sharks which had to rob the old man of his fish; made them all and loved them all and pitied them all. It's all right. Praise God that whatever made and loves and pities Hemingway and me kept him from touching it any further.[4]

Faulkner claims that the pity Hemingway plays with in *The Sun Also Rises* is mastered in *The Old Man and the Sea*. The reader feels pity for Santiago because he worked so long catching the fish only to bring back the fish's skeleton. However, Santiago does not feel pity for himself.

When the first group of sharks start tearing up his record-setting marlin, Santiago talks to himself:

> It was too good to last, he thought. I wish it had been a dream now and that I had never hooked the fish and was alone in bed on the newspapers.
>
> "But man is not made for defeat," he said. "A man can be destroyed but not defeated."[5]

By bringing back a marlin that is little more than a skeleton, he is destroyed. After struggling with the huge fish for two days, he has hardly any meat to sell. He is not defeated, however, because he knows he fought a good fight, and he won.

Actually, Santiago feels pity for the marlin. He does not give in to feeling sorry for himself. That is his dignity. After the second bunch of sharks come and eat the marlin he caught, Santiago says, "I wish it were a dream and that I had never hooked him. I'm sorry about it, fish. It makes everything wrong."[6] If Santiago had felt pity for himself, it would have been all wrong. Faulkner writes "It's all right" because feeling sorry for oneself means being defeated. Santiago is not defeated.

This is the key idea of *The Old Man and the Sea*. The simple story of Santiago losing his fish is an allegory of people suffering defeat. Although some other fishermen laugh at Santiago for having such bad luck fishing, Santiago remains dignified. He does not talk meanly to those fishermen; he merely hopes he will catch a fish the next day. He is proud at how perfect he keeps his fishing lines, and he has certain ways of doing things.

Santiago loves the ocean and treats nature like people:

> He was very fond of flying fish as they were his principal friends on the ocean. He was sorry for the birds, especially the small delicate dark terns that were always flying and looking and almost never finding, and he thought, the birds have a harder life than we do except for the robber birds and the heavy strong ones. Why did they make birds so delicate and fine as those sea swallows when the ocean can be so cruel?[7]

This is an example of irony in nature. Santiago wonders how the sea can be so beautiful and kind and also so cruel and wicked. He thinks it is because that is the sea's nature, and she (the sea) cannot help it.

ALLUSIONS

Santiago makes his way back to the harbor in the darkness, and there is no one to help him dock his boat. He ties his boat to a rock, removes the mast, and begins to carry it on his shoulder back to his shack. As he carries the mast up the hill, he stumbles and has to rest. He puts the mast back on his shoulder and tries to walk on. This simple scene could be an allusion with deep meaning.

An allusion is a reference in a book or story to a scene, person, or event in another book or story. If something in one book seems a lot like something in another book, the character or event in the newer book could be an allusion to the older book. For example, in a short story called "Nobody Ever Dies," the sister of two soldiers is chased down and caught by the enemy. Her name is Maria. They put her in the back seat of a car to take her in for questioning. Hemingway writes:

ALLUSION— *A writing device in which a scene, person, or event in one book or story refers to a similar thing in another book or story.*

> She sat there holding herself very still against the back of the seat. She seemed now to have a strange confidence. It was the same confidence

another girl her age had felt a little more than five hundred years before in the market place of a town called Rouen. . . . The two girls named Jeanne and Maria had nothing in common except this sudden strange confidence which came when they needed it.[8]

This is an allusion to the life of Joan of Arc (in French it is Jeanne d'Arc). In 1431, Joan of Arc was burned at the stake in the Old Market Square in Rouen, France, because she decided to listen to what she thought were saints talking to her rather than do what the king or Church officials said. Maria will most likely be tortured and suffer a death not that different from Joan of Arc's. Maria's situation is an allusion to Joan of Arc's situation 500 years earlier.

In *The Old Man and the Sea* an old sailor risks everything to pursue a mysterious sea creature, a storyline similar to that of *Moby Dick. The Old Man*

MOBY DICK

Moby Dick (1851) is a novel by Herman Melville, centering on the character Captain Ahab and his quest to destroy the great, white whale, Moby Dick. On the surface, the novel brilliantly captures the exciting and dramatic life aboard a nineteenth-century whaling ship. On another level, however, *Moby Dick* is a deep allegory, with the whale symbolizing the mysterious forces of the universe, and Captain Ahab representing the human struggle to understand and conquer those forces.

and the Sea was published almost exactly 100 years after *Moby Dick*. Therefore, one could say the basic storyline of *The Old Man and the Sea* is an allusion to *Moby Dick*.

Santiago carrying the mast on his shoulder can be seen as an allusion to the scene in the New Testament of the Bible where Jesus carries the cross that he is to be crucified upon. Hemingway compares Santiago with Jesus Christ. Both men suffered but were not totally defeated. Both men were fishermen. And both men were surrounded by people who did not believe in them.

Hemingway makes the allusion to Jesus clear in this scene when Santiago sees more sharks coming to attack his marlin: "'Ay,'" he said aloud. There is no translation for this word and perhaps it is just a noise such as a man might make, involuntarily, feeling the nail go through his hands and into the wood."[9]

This description could allude to Jesus, and the wood could be the cross he was crucified on. A reader must be careful not to think that Hemingway definitely wrote *The Old Man and the Sea* to be a Christian allegory, because other readers might find a different allegory. When thinking about what symbols in literature mean, it is important to provide evidence to support your interpretation. The many interpretations of literature are part of what makes good writing so interesting.

Both Jesus and Santiago were destroyed but not defeated. The last years of Ernest Hemingway's life slowly destroyed this great writer, with the final destruction coming from within.

SELF-
DESTRUCTION

The Final Years of Ernest Hemingway

The transition from a young boy in Illinois writing silly poems about football teams to America's most famous writer was not without its rough spots. Along the way, Ernest Hemingway had made many enemies, wasted much money, and almost wore himself out. He had built a very distinctive image for himself and his writing, and many people are still unsure where Ernest Hemingway ends and his characters begin. There are pieces of him and his acquaintances throughout his writing.

Hemingway played as hard as he worked, and this became harder to do as he aged. He was no longer a teenage cub reporter for the Kansas City *Star*. Still, he enjoyed parties with other writers, long meals with his friends, and longer days fishing aboard the *Pilar*.

In 1953, Ernest and Mary Hemingway went

on another African safari to celebrate Ernest's recent writing successes. He was making a lot of money by having his books made into movies, and *The Old Man and the Sea* was still selling like crazy. In fact, that book won him the Pulitzer Prize for 1952. In Africa, Hemingway hunted big game and enjoyed the fresh air. However, the Hemingways were in *two* airplane accidents. Word got out, and some newspapers published the news that Ernest Hemingway and his wife were killed in a plane wreck.

Interestingly, the very famous American writer Mark Twain had the news of his death published before he actually died. Hemingway greatly admired Mark Twain, and in his 1935 book *Green Hills of Africa*, he wrote, "All Modern American literature comes from one book by Mark Twain called Huckleberry Finn."[1] There are many similarities between the lives and writing of Mark Twain and Ernest Hemingway.

Ernest and Mary Hemingway survived both crashes, but Ernest was badly wounded. He used his head as a battering ram to bust open the jammed door of the burning airplane. Surviving two airplane crashes in Africa helped build his image as an indestructible superman, but his head was badly injured, and he suffered injuries to his liver, spine, and arms. He also suffered burns. Hemingway tried to hide the pain his injuries caused him, but he moved much slower. He was in pain much of the time. The plane wrecks slowed his thinking and writing, and that depressed him.

THE NOBEL PRIZE

Hemingway's spirits were lifted, however, when he was awarded the Nobel Prize for Literature in 1954. He was too ill to go to the awards ceremony, but he wrote a speech that someone else read. In his speech, Hemingway wrote, "A writer should write what he has to say and not speak it."[2] In other words, good writing is not like listening to a storyteller. Good writing should allow the reader to hear the story in his or her own voice. The author's voice should be silent. Many other authors and poets (notably T. S. Eliot) agreed with this idea—that good writing lets the reader forget about the writer and lose themselves in the actual story.

In his acceptance speech, Hemingway also wrote that writing is a lonely business. A writer

Ernest Hemingway and his fourth wife, Mary, are pictured here during the mid-1950s.

has to do a lot of thinking, and a writer has to work alone. The reward of completing a complicated chapter or describing a certain event in the best words is hard to communicate to someone else, so many of the rewards of being a writer are for the writer only. It is hard to share that feeling of accomplishment.

Hemingway grew more and more sick throughout the late 1950s. Years of heavy alcohol drinking and numerous accidents weakened his body, but he tried to continue writing. He began rewriting a long novel he had started several years earlier.

The Hemingways eventually bought a house in Ketcham, Idaho. Hemingway thought Ketcham would be a good place to relax, write, and enjoy nature. In the summer of 1959, Ernest and Mary Hemingway sailed to Spain one last time. Some scholars call this "the dangerous summer" for several reasons: some of Hemingway's bullfighter friends were severely injured, Hemingway worked and partied to exhaustion, and his depression deepened. The Hemingway marriage also grew strained, and Hemingway was having financial difficulties.

But Hemingway felt the need to continue

writing. He did not want the public to think he was washed up as a writer. He had always demanded the best of himself, and he did not want to let himself or his readers down. Writing had become a part of his life; he could not survive without it.

FINAL DAYS

By 1960, Ernest Hemingway's health was quite bad. In addition to his physical injuries and complaints, his mind seems to have been slipping. He began to think the FBI and other officials were spying on him. He was admitted to the hospital twice for psychiatric treatment, but he was allowed to return to his Ketchum, Idaho, house with his wife, Mary.

At the hospital, Hemingway underwent electroshock therapy. This all but destroyed his ability to write. For a man whose adult life was shaped by his writing, this must have been a terrible time. Occasionally, Hemingway seemed almost like his old self, but most of the time he was paranoid and depressed. Mary did what she could to help him feel better, but Ernest had always been an independent man.

Hemingway shoos away his pet cat as he tries to get some work done on his typewriter.

He thought about suicide, and his friends and his wife caught him more than once holding a gun as if he were going to shoot himself. By the middle of 1961, Ernest Hemingway was certainly not his old self. He could not concentrate, and he was terribly upset that he could no longer think clearly enough to write.

THE END OF A LIFE

Early on the Sunday morning of July 2, 1961, Ernest Hemingway woke up before Mary. He loaded one of his favorite shotguns, and he killed himself. He was buried in Ketchum, Idaho. Ernest Hemingway's three sons and three of his four sisters attended the funeral.

In his will, Hemingway instructed that his personal letters be destroyed, and most of them were. Many letters and drafts of stories survived, however, and are held in a few libraries across America. Correspondence stored in his Cuba home was recently released to American researchers, who are carefully cataloging letters.

The same hunger for adventure and desire to write that fueled Ernest Hemingway for so many years were part of his eventual self-destruction.

CHAPTER 8

LITERARY AFTERGLOW

The Hemingway Legacy

Even though Ernest Hemingway asked his wife Mary to burn all his letters and notes when he died, several books by Hemingway were published after his death. These books were not finished by Hemingway, but were put together either by family members or editors. The titles of some of the books published after his death are *A Moveable Feast* (published in 1964), *Islands in the Stream* (1970), *Hemingway's Selected Letters 1917–1961* (1981), *The Garden of Eden* (1986), and *True at First Light* (1999).

Scholars, students, and researchers continue to study Hemingway's writing style and to enjoy his writing. Hemingway was an exceptional person. He had adventures most people can only imagine, but he created stories and characters we can all enjoy. From his earliest poems to his newspaper articles to his posthumous novels, his writing is real. It is not about a romanticized or ideal world but the real world. His writing is as sacred as it is profane, as joyful as it is depressing.

THE JOY OF HEMINGWAY

The joy in Hemingway's writing may be found in his basic enjoyment of life. The feel of icy cold water in a trout stream, the taste of pasta asciutta on the battlefield, the sight of lions on the beach in Africa, the sound of silk worms eating mulberry leaves—they are all signs of life. Things are not always good, and sometimes bad things happen to good people. Still, we live to stay true to our code and try to help others. This is a message in Hemingway's writing.

He believed that writing is a lonely business, but he also believed that people cannot live without other people. Nick Adams goes to the Big Two-Hearted River to be alone, but his character bears the traces of people he knew. Frederic Henry and Catherine Barkley, and Robert Jordan and Maria are couples that loved each other so much that they felt as though they were one person. Jordan says to Maria, "You are also me now. . . . Thou art me too now."[1] The code hero never

Ernest Hemingway at work at the writing table.
Hemingway later lamented the lonely existence
of the writer.

gives up, and Ernest Hemingway gave up only once—that Sunday morning in 1961.

Hemingway forever changed American literature. The bridges he built have held. Hemingway began writing in a style that is quite common now. All endings don't have to be happy ones where all problems are solved; not all heroes have to be perfect in every way; not all good people are rewarded; and not all bad people are punished.

THE HEMINGWAY STYLE

Hemingway wrote about characters who are not really connected with any bigger group. The characters with dignity are usually not connected with a political party or even a particular country. This idea was rather new in literature, and it was a major idea in Modernism.

As populations grew and the world became more and more busy, the individual seemed lost. Many writers before Hemingway looked at groups of people—nationalities, social groups, and armies. Hemingway wrote about one person in an army or one man on the sea. Not just that, Hemingway wrote about what that one person thinks and what it is like when the battle is over or the hero returns home with the mere skeleton of a big catch.

In *A Moveable Feast*, Hemingway wrote about how he did his actual writing when he lived in Paris:

> I always worked until I had something done and I always stopped when I knew what was going to happen next. That way I could be sure of going on the next day. But sometimes when I was starting a new story and I could not get it going, I would sit in front of the fire and squeeze the peel of the little oranges into the edge of the flame and watch the sputter of blue that they made. I would stand and look over the roofs of Paris and think, "Do not worry. You have always written before and you will write now. All you have to do is write one true sentence. Write the truest sentence that you know."[2]

He wrote about what he thought was true and real. This was not always an easy assignment for Hemingway, and he felt extremely happy after he had written.

In that same book he writes, "There is never any ending to Paris and the memory of each person who has lived in it differs from that of any other."[3]

ONE TRUE SENTENCE

Hemingway's idea of one true sentence works like what he says about memories of Paris. What one person believes is true might not work for another person. Ernest Hemingway wrote in a very factual manner so that readers can "fill in" color and extra detail as they want. It does not matter if the year is 1926 or 2026; his writing will still have meaning for readers who put forth the effort to read carefully and think about what they have read. Even though Ernest Hemingway is considered to be part of the Lost Generation, his writing is timeless.

THE HEMINGWAY LEGACY

Ernest Hemingway's residences in Oak Park, Illinois; Paris, France; Key West, Florida; outside Havana, Cuba; Ketcham, Idaho; and other places are tourist destinations now. They have been preserved to give visitors the feeling that Hemingway is alive, just upstairs preparing for another writing session. Maybe he is seated at his desk, pondering one true sentence to begin a new novel. Maybe he is on the veranda, sipping wine in celebration of another 12-page day.

Although Ernest Hemingway is gone, his personality and writing are still with us. His writing style changed American literature forever. The short declarative sentence, the principle of the iceberg, and Hemingway's use of pity and irony is the foundation upon which today's fiction is built.

CHRONOLOGY

1899—*July 21*: Ernest Miller Hemingway born in Oak Park, Illinois.

1914—*August*: World War I begins in Europe.

1917—*June*: Graduates from Oak Park High School. Moves to Kansas City to work as a reporter for the Kansas City *Star*.
November: United States enters World War I.

1918—Begins service as an ambulance driver in Italy for the Red Cross.
July 8: Seriously wounded in Fossalta, Italy. Begins romance with his nurse, Agnes von Kurowsky.
November 11: Germany accepts armistice, ending World War I.

1919—Returns to Oak Park as a war hero; Agnes von Kurowsky breaks off relationship.

1920—Moves to Chicago; finds work as a writer and editor.

1921—*September 3*: Marries Hadley Richardson.
Leaves for Paris, France, to work as a foreign correspondent for the *The Toronto Star* newspaper.

1923—*August*: *Three Stories and Ten Poems* published.
in our time is published.

October 10: Son, John Hadley Nicanor Hemingway ("Bumby") is born.

1925—*October*: *In Our Time* published.

1926—*March*: *The Torrents of Spring* published.
May: *The Sun Also Rises* published.
August: Legally separated from Hadley.

1927—*May 10*: Marries Pauline Pfeiffer.

1928—*June 28*: Son, Patrick Hemingway, is born.
December 6: Father, Clarence Hemingway, commits suicide.

1929—*September*: *A Farewell to Arms* published.
October: U.S. stock market crashes; Great Depression begins.

1931—Moves to Key West, Florida.
November 12: Son, Gregory Hancock Hemingway, is born.

1932—*September*: *Death in the Afternoon* published.

1933—Goes on first African safari with wife Pauline.
Winner Take Nothing published.

1935—*October*: *Green Hills of Africa* published.

1936—*July*: Spanish Civil War begins.

1937—*July*: *To Have and Have Not* published.
Covers Spanish Civil War as correspondent.

1938—Publishes the play, *The Fifth Column*.

1939—*April*: Spanish Civil War ends; General Francisco Franco becomes dictator of Spain.
September: World War II begins in Europe.
December: Legally separated from Pauline.

1940—*October*: *For Whom the Bell Tolls* published.
November 21: Marries Martha Gellhorn.

1941—Goes to China to cover the Chinese–Japanese War.
December: U.S. enters World War II.

1942—Patrols Cuban waters, searching for German U-boats.

1944—Works as war correspondent in Europe; witnesses D-Day landing on Omaha Beach.

1945—*June*: World War II ends.
December 21: Divorced from Martha.

1946—*March 14*: Marries Mary Welsh.

1950—*September*: *Across the River and into the Trees* published.

1951—*June 28*: Mother, Grace Hemingway, dies.

1952—*September*: *The Old Man and the Sea* published after being serialized in *Life* magazine.

1953—*May*: Awarded Pulitzer Prize for *The Old Man and the Sea*.

1954—Suffers injuries in two separate plane crashes.
October: Awarded Nobel Prize in Literature.

1957—Begins work on *A Moveable Feast*.

1960—Leaves Cuba due to political changes; moves to Idaho.

1961—*July 1*: Commits suicide in Ketchum, Idaho.

1964—*A Moveable Feast* published.

1970—*Islands in the Stream* published.

1986—*The Garden of Eden* published.

1999—*True at First Light* published.

Chapter Notes

Chapter 1. The Lost Generation

1. Ernest Hemingway, in *The Complete Short Stories* (New York: Quality Paperback Book Club, 1993), p. 206.

2. Ernest Hemingway, *A Moveable Feast* (New York: Scribner's, 1964), p. 29.

3. Ernest Hemingway, *By-Line*, ed. William White (New York: Simon & Schuster, 1998), p. 219.

4. Ernest Hemingway, *The Sun Also Rises* (New York: Quality Paperback Book Club, 1993), p. 114.

5. Ernest Hemingway, *A Farewell to Arms* (New York: Quality Paperback Book Club, 1993), p. 185.

6. Ernest Hemingway, *In Our Time* (New York: Scribner's, 1958), p. 177.

7. Ibid., p. 179.

Chapter 2. 'Fraid a Nothing!

1. Carlos Baker, *Ernest Hemingway: The Writer as Artist* (Princeton, N.J.: Princeton University Press, 1990), p. 5. Also in James R. Mellow, *Hemingway: A Life Without Consequences* (New York: Houghton Mifflin, 1992), p. 6.

2. Pam Johnson, "Making Values Visible," *Poynter Online*, November 11, 2002, <http://www.poynter.org/columns.asp?id=34&aid=9101> (December 6, 2004).

3. Ernest Hemingway, "Night Before Battle," *The Complete Short Stories* (New York: Quality Paperback Book Club, 1993), p. 437.

4. Ernest Hemingway, *A Moveable Feast*, p. 12.

5. Ernest Hemingway, *Complete Poems*, ed. Nicholas Gerogiannis (Lincoln, Neb.: University of Nebraska Press, 1992), p. xxiii.

CHAPTER 3. *IN OUR TIME*

1. Ernest Hemingway, *In Our Time* (New York: Scribner's, 1958), p. 175.

2. Ibid., p. 213.

3. James R. Mellow, *Hemingway: A Life Without Consequences* (New York: Houghton Mifflin), p. xx.

4. Ernest Hemingway, *For Whom the Bell Tolls*, p. 73.

5. Ibid., p. 169.

6. Ernest Hemingway, unpublished draft of *A Farewell to Arms* (Item #168 in The Hemingway Collection, JFK Library in Boston, Mass.).

7. Ernest Hemingway, *A Farewell to Arms* (New York: Quality Paperback Book Club, 1993), p. 243.

8. Hemingway, *In Our Time*, p. 81.

9. Ernest Hemingway, *The Complete Short Stories* (New York: Quality Paperback Book Club), p. 221.

10. Hemingway, *In Our Time*, p. 21.

11. Ibid.

12. Ibid., p. 211.

CHAPTER 4. HOPE IN THE FUTILITY

1. Ernest Hemingway, *In Our Time* (New York: Scribner's, 1958), pp. 146–147.

2. Ibid., p.147.

3. Ibid., p. 212.

4. Ernest Hemingway, *The Complete Short Stories* (New York: Quality Paperback Book Club, 1993), p. 291.

5. Ibid.

6. Ernest Hemingway, *The Sun Also Rises* (New York: Quality Paperback Book Club, 1993), p. 11.

7. Ibid., p. 31.

8. Ibid., p. 55.

9. Ibid., p. 247.

CHAPTER 5. TO WAR

1. Carlos Baker, *Ernest Hemingway: Selected Letters* (London: Granada, 1972), p. 176.

2. James R. Mellow, *Hemingway: A Life Without Consequences*, p. 379.

3. Ernest Hemingway, *A Farewell to Arms* (New York: Quality Paperback Book Club, 1993), p. 3.

4. Ibid., p. 4.

5. Ibid., p. 184.

6. Ernest Hemingway, "The Short, Happy Life of Francis Macomber," *The Complete Short Stories* (New York: Quality Paperback Book Club, 1993), p. 27.

7. Ibid., p. 6.

8. Ibid.

9. Ibid.

10. Ibid.

11. Ibid., p. 21.

12. Carlos Baker, *Ernest Hemingway: A Life Story* (New York: Scribner Book Company, 1999), p. 339.

13. John Donne, *Devotions Upon Emergent Occasions* (London: McGill-Queen's University Press, 1975), p. 87.

14. Ernest Hemingway, *For Whom the Bell Tolls* (New York: Quality Paperback Book Club, 1993), p. 41.

15. Ibid., p. 466.

16. Ibid., p. 15.

17. Ibid., p. 267.

18. Ibid., p. 166.

19. Carlos Baker, *Ernest Hemingway: A Life Story,* p. 363.

CHAPTER 6. DESTROYED BUT NOT DEFEATED

1. Ernest Hemingway, *The Old Man and the Sea* (New York: Scribner, 1995), p. 14.

2. Ibid., p. 12.

3. Ernest Hemingway, *The Complete Short Stories* (New York: Quality Paperback Book Club, 1993), p. 431.

4. Carlos Baker, *Ernest Hemingway: A Life Story* (New York: Scribner Book Company, 1999), p. 504.

5. Ernest Hemingway, *The Old Man and the Sea,* p. 103.

6. Ibid., p. 110.

7. Ibid., p. 29.

8. Hemingway, *The Complete Short Stories,* p. 480.

9. Ernest Hemingway, *The Old Man and the Sea*, p. 107.

CHAPTER 7. SELF-DESTRUCTION

1. Ernest Hemingway, *Green Hills of Africa* (New York: Scribners, 1935), p. 22.

2. Ernest Hemingway, "Ernest Hemingway—Banquet Speech," *Nobelprize.org*, n.d., <http://nobelprize.org/literature/laureates/1954/hemingway-speech.html> (December 7, 2004).

CHAPTER 8. LITERARY AFTERGLOW

1. Ernest Hemingway, *For Whom the Bell Tolls,* (New York: Quality Paperback Book Club, 1993) pp. 463–464.

2. Ernest Hemingway, *A Moveable Feast*, (New York: Scribner's, 1964) p. 12.

3. Ibid, p. 209.

GLOSSARY

allegory—A writing device in which a person, object, or event has more than one meaning. The incident of Santiago and the marlin in *The Old Man and the Sea* could be an allegory of the life of Jesus Christ.

allusion—A writing device in which a scene, person, or event in one book or story refers to a similar thing in another book or story. For example, parts of *The Old Man and the Sea* can be seen as allusions to *Moby Dick*.

Code hero—A type of Hemingway character who is confident in his beliefs and shows "grace under pressure." He lives by a set of rules and never compromises those rules.

fascism—A type of government that encourages nationalism over individuality. A severe leader usually leads it, and people who speak out against the government are quieted.

futility—The feeling of helplessness; a feeling that results cannot be predicted or expected.

irony—There are two types of irony: when a word or words are used to express an idea that is opposite that of the words' literal meaning, and when the actual outcome of events is different from what was expected. In modernism, this often involves the idea of humans being rewarded and punished at random.

Lost Generation, The—A group of writers who gained fame between World War I and the 1930s. They wrote about the rootlessness, futility, and alienation they felt.

Modernism—In literature, an era when writers wanted to break from the style of the past to explore new ways of writing. The movement is a little different in Europe and America, but it could be said to span from 1900 to 1960. The era signalled a shift toward more realistic writing.

nihilism—The belief that human existence is completely pointless and useless.

parody—A work in which one writer imitates and exaggerates another writer's work.

pity—Feeling sadness for the suffering of another.

realism—Writing that emphasizes people and situations that are more true to everyday life.

Romantic literature—Writing that emphasizes passion and imagination over realism.

symbol—Something that represents or suggests another person or thing.

symbolism—The representation of things by use of symbols.

theme—A distinctive quality or concern in one or more works of fiction.

Victorian era—Time spanning the reign of Queen Victoria (1837–1901). The literature of this era moved away from moral righteousness to explore the struggle between the rich and the poor as well as the conflict between religion and science.

MAJOR WORKS BY ERNEST HEMINGWAY

Three Stories and Ten Poems (1923)

in our time (1923)

In Our Time (1925)

The Torrents of Spring (1926)

Men Without Women (1927)

A Farewell to Arms (1929)

Death in the Afternoon (1932)

Winner Take Nothing (1933)

Green Hills of Africa (1935)

To Have and Have Not (1937)

The Spanish Earth (1938)

The Fifth Column and the First Forty-Nine Stories (1938)

For Whom the Bell Tolls (1940)

Men at War [edited by Hemingway] (1942)

Across the River and into the Trees (1950)

The Old Man and the Sea (1952)

A Moveable Feast (1964)

MAJOR WORKS BY ERNEST HEMINGWAY

By-Line: Ernest Hemingway (1967)
Islands in the Stream (1970)
The Nick Adams Stories (1972)
Complete Poems (1979)
The Garden of Eden (1986)
True at First Light (1999)

FURTHER READING

Bloom, Harold. *Ernest Hemingway*. Broomall, Pa.: Chelsea House, 2001.

Marshe, Carole. *Ernest Hemingway*. Peachtree City, Ga.: Gallopade International, 2002.

Oliver, Charles M. *Ernest Hemingway A to Z: The Essential Reference to His Life & Work*. New York: Facts on File, 1999.

Russell, Frazier. *Ernest Hemingway: Romantic Adventurer*. Kipling Press, 1998.

Weisbrod, Eva. *A Student's Guide to F. Scott Fitzgerald*. Berkeley Heights, N.J.: Enslow Publishers, Inc., 2004.

Yannuzzi, Della A. *Ernest Hemingway: Writer and Adventurer*. Berkeley Heights, N.J.: Enslow Publishers, Inc., 1998.

INTERNET ADDRESSES

The Hemingway Society
http://www.hemingwaysociety.org

The Hemingway Resource Center
http://www.lostgeneration.com/hrc.htm

Internet Public Library—Online Literary Criticism Collection
http://www.ipl.org.ar/ref/litcrit/

INDEX